# DOWN-HOME
# CAJUN COOKING
# FAVORITES

## by Neal Bertrand

Cypress Cove Publishing

Visit our website for new items and free recipes:
www.CypressCovePublishing.com

CYPRESS COVE PUBLISHING
ATTN: Neal Bertrand
908 Amilcar Blvd.
Lafayette, LA 70501

Revised second edition, ISBN: 978-0-9705868-7-2
Library of Congress Control Number: 2010913399

## About the front cover:

This mouth-watering dish of crawfish étouffée is one of the
all-time favorite recipes of Cajun Country.
Look for the recipe on page 60.

Author and Executive Editor, Neal Bertrand
Crawfish étouffée styled by Sandra Day, food stylist, Lafayette,
Louisiana
Front cover photography by Doug Dugas, Lafayette, Louisiana
Back cover photo courtesy of Danny Izzo, Nouveau Photeau,
Lafayette, Louisiana
Book design and production by Jeremy Bertrand, Cypress Cove
Publishing

# Acknowledgements

### *We wish to thank:*

Mr. Carroll Conques for his inspiration to start this project.

Mrs. Bonnie Gotte for the use of old recipes handed down for generations from family members in Acadia and Jeff Davis parishes.

Mrs. Connie Monies Gremillion for the use of some of the recipes from *First You Say Grace*, a cookbook compiled by family and friends of Cathedral-Carmel school in Lafayette, La.

Mrs. Bootsie John Landry for letting us use some recipes from her book, *The Best of South Louisiana Cooking*.

Chef John Folse, Chef Alex Patout, and Riviana Foods for permission to reprint their recipes.

Charley & Ruth Addison, for the use of a few of the recipes from their book, *Cooking With Crazy Charley Part 3*.

Mr. Robert Bordelon, for contributing some very old, classic Cajun recipes.

Mr. Keith Barras for the use of recipes from *Granny's Cajun Cookin'*.

Mrs. Junior Lagneaux of Lagneaux's Restaurant on Ridge Road in Lafayette, for the use of some of their delicious, classic Cajun recipes served in their restaurant for decades.

Ms. Michelle Lemoine, and Ms. Deniese Zeringue, Associate Extension Agents with the LSU AgCenter, Cooperative Extension Service, Evangeline and St. Charles Parishes, respectively.

Mr. Don Chachere for the use of recipes from *Tony Chachere's Cajun Country Cookbook*.

My Dad and Mom, Curtis and Edmay Bertrand, for all the great food and wonderful smells coming from the kitchen when my sister Karen and I were growing up in Opelousas.

Doug Dugas, for a beautiful photograph for the front cover.
Sandra Day, for making the food smile for the camera.

Neal Bertrand, Author and Publisher

# CONTENTS

# FOREWORD

## By Sandra Day

When my out-of-town friends come to visit me in Lafayette, one of the things I'm most eager to show them is our food here in south Louisiana. I take them to my favorite plate lunch spots, to our smoke-scented meat markets, and to the Cajun section of our grocery stores. I give them what I've come to call my "Cajun culinary tour," which, of course, includes some of our beautiful Louisiana landscapes, too. If there's time, we spend a few hours in my kitchen cooking up something savory ... a chicken and andouille gumbo, a crawfish stew, or perhaps some corn maque choux.

In all the tours I've done, whether for a professional food and travel editor or a novice in the kitchen, I've never failed to see a sense of delight at the incredible cuisine we have here: the gumbos, poboys, étouffées, sausages, fricassées, jambalayas, sauce piquantes, and boiled and fried seafood.

In essence, *Down-Home Cajun Cooking Favorites* is like taking a culinary tour of Cajun country. The publisher has carefully selected these recipes from good cooks across the region. Most of the contributors are home cooks ... ma-mères and pa-pères, t-tantes and t-noncs, who have been making these recipes day in and day out, year after year, for decades. They assume that everyone knows how to make a roux, how to tell when a gumbo has simmered long enough, and how peppered a sauce piquante should be. With the exception of a couple of spicier dishes, Cajun food should not be overly hot; it should be well seasoned and lightly peppered.

In my many years as a newspaper and magazine food editor, I've learned what it takes to make a good food story, a good recipe, and a good cookbook. They all begin with a good cook, and you'll find many of them in these pages.

# INTRODUCTION

"Cajun Country" is a region in south Louisiana known for its rich culture and mouth-watering dishes. It stretches over a 22-parish region called Acadiana. The characteristics of this rich culture are that of warmth, the joy of life, and the bond of family.

The Acadians first came to south Louisiana after being exiled from Nova Scotia, then called Acadie. They brought with them the love of family, fellowship and good food. The elders here share stories of days passed, and the Cajun-French language is still strong amongst them. French Immersion Schools attempt to preserve the French language in their young. Families gather around crawfish boils, gumbo dinners, and boucheries…the coming together of generations, bridging the gap around the family table.

## Introduction to Revised Second Edition

I wanted to make a few changes to some recipes in the book, but it seems I never had the time. Then one day I met a young couple who love to cook, Cliff and Amy Amox from Arnaudville, in St. Landry Parish, Louisiana. They agreed to help, so I chose the recipes that needed to be improved and they kitchen-tested them. To my delight they all tasted wonderful!

Some recipes are new, others are adjusted. They are: Boudin, Cracklins, Shrimp Bisque, Cajun Corn Soup, Chicken, Sausage & Okra Gumbo, Shrimp & Okra Gumbo, Crab Étouffée, Crawfish Jambalaya in a Rice Cooker, Seafood Jambalaya in a Rice Cooker, Couche-Couche, Rice Dressing (Dirty Rice), and Smothered Cabbage; plus all of the Sweets & Treats were kitchen tested and perfected by them, to their culinary delight.

Enjoy!
Neal Bertrand, Executive Editor & Publisher

# Pronunciation Guide to Cajun Food Names

**Andouille** = ahn-DOO-we
**Au Gratin** = oh-gra-tan; Gra rhymes with bra; the "n" on tan is silent
**Beignets** = bain-YAY
**Bisque** = bisk
**Boudin** = BOO-dan, the "n" is silent
**Bouillabaisse** = boo-ya BASE
**Couche-Couche** = koosh-koosh
**Courtbouillon** = COO-be yawn, the "n" is silent
**Graton** = Gra rhymes with bra; ton rhymes with gone, the "n" is silent
**Croquettes** = kro-kets
**Étouffée** = A-too FAY
**Fricassée** = FREAK-a-say
**Jambalaya** = jum-ba-LIE-ya
**Les Oreilles de Cochon** = lays o-RAY de koe-shon; the "n" is silent
**Maque Choux** = mock shoe
**Mirlitons** = mir-lee tons; the "n" is silent
**Pain Perdu** = pan (the "n" is silent) pair-doo
**Paté de Fois Gras** = pot-TAY de FWAH  graw
**Pecan Pralines** = p'CONE PRAH-leans; <u>not</u> PEE-can PRAY-leans
**Roux** = roo
**Sauce Piquante** = sos pee-KAHNT
**Tasso** = TAH-so
**Yam Pie de Louisianne** = loo-WEE-zee-ANNE

# BOUDIN

3 1/2 lbs. boneless pork butt (stew meat),  cut in pieces
1/4 lb. pork liver
2 tbsp. salt, divided
2 tbsp. red pepper, divided
2 tbsp. black pepper, divided
1/2 onion, coarsely chopped
1/2 bell pepper, coarsely chopped

1 bulb garlic (8 or 9 cloves)
4 sprigs fresh parsley
2 stalks fresh celery
Water
3 1/4 cups (26 oz.) uncooked rice
1 cup chopped green onion
1 tbsp. Kitchen Bouquet
1 tbsp. paprika

1. Season meat with one tbsp. each of salt, red and black pepper; add meat and next five vegetables to a large gumbo pot.
2. Add water until it is 2 inches above ingredients. Cook on high for 1 to 1 1/2 hours.
3. Cook the rice.
4. When meat is done, drain all liquid from pot and reserve.
5. Grind meat and vegetables using a coarse grinding plate, (about 3/8-diameter holes.)
6. Add rice and green onion to meat mixture; stir in enough reserved liquid to make it mushy. Stir well. To get the right consistency the meat mixture should jiggle when shaken.
7. Season this mixture with remaining one tbsp. salt and peppers.
8. Add Kitchen Bouquet and paprika for enhanced flavor and color.
9. Put into a boudin casing or eat as a dressing.
– Cliff Amox
Arnaudville, La.

# CRACKLINS (GRATONS)

Editor's note: I watched the butchers make cracklins to be sold in their market. They cooked 60 pounds of pork bellies in a huge pot, stirring it with a long metal paddle. It made 20 pounds of cracklins when done. You can follow the same process at home with a smaller amount of meat. You will need a meat thermometer and propane burner setup. This must be cooked outside.

**Enough cooking oil or hog lard to bring to 1-inch depth**
**Pork bellies cut into 2 or 3-inch chunks**
**Seasoning**

1. Add oil or hog lard to a large Dutch oven pot. Get temperature to 180 to 220 degrees, then add meat. Pot should remain uncovered.
2. Keep at a rolling boil. The fat on the meat will slowly melt away and the meat will sink. Stir often so it does not stick to the pot.
3. After a long while the meat will begin to float and the skin will start blistering or "blooming." Once the oil gets to 310 degrees take them out of the pot and cool to room temperature.
4. Heat the grease back up to 380 degrees and put the cracklins back in for seven minutes. This will cause the cracklins to "pop". Then take out and season immediately.
− Cliff Amox and Jacque Leger
St. Landry Parish, La.

# CHUNKY BOUDIN BALLS

| | |
|---|---|
| **1 egg** | **Italian breadcrumbs** |
| **1/2 cup milk** | **Cooking oil for deep frying** |
| **1 lb. boudin** | |

1. Mix egg and milk in a small bowl.
2. Remove casing from boudin and roll into one-inch balls.
3. Dip in milk and egg mixture, then roll in breadcrumbs and fry in oil.
4. Drain on paper towels and serve hot.
− Ethel Bergeaux

# CRAB CROQUETTES

3 tbsp. melted butter
1 beaten egg
1 onion, chopped fine
3 cloves garlic, chopped fine
Cayenne pepper and salt, to taste

3 tbsp. flour
1 box frozen crabmeat, picked over for shells and cartilage
Breadcrumbs
Cooking oil for deep frying

1. Combine all ingredients except breadcrumbs and oil and mix well; form into balls.
2. Roll balls or croquettes in breadcrumbs and fry in hot oil until golden brown.
– Marie Olivier

# CRAWFISH DIP

1 medium onion, chopped
2 cloves garlic, minced
2 stalks celery, chopped
1 bell pepper, chopped
1 1/2 sticks butter or margarine
1/3 cup flour

2 lbs. peeled and deveined crawfish or shrimp, chopped
1 lb. Mexican hot Velveeta cheese
2 tbsp. chopped parsley
1 bunch green onions, chopped
1/3 to 1/2 cup half-and-half

1. Sauté vegetables in butter on low heat.
2. When vegetables are wilted, add flour and stir until it is completely dissolved to make a paste.
3. Add crawfish or shrimp and cook on low heat for about 5 minutes.
4. Cut the Velveeta into large chunks and add to mixture; stir until melted.
5. Add parsley and chopped green onions.
6. Add half-and-half to desired consistency and mix well.
Serve with crackers or chips.
– Joyce Solari

# CRAWFISH PIES

1 cup chopped onion
1/2 cup chopped bell pepper
1/2 cup chopped celery
4 large cloves garlic, chopped
1 stick margarine

1 lb. crawfish, with fat
Salt and red pepper, to taste
3 slices American processed cheese
1/2 cup chopped green onion tops
1/8 cup parsley flakes

**1/4 cup Italian breadcrumbs**  **16 (3-inch) frozen tart shells, defrosted**

1. In a heavy saucepan, over medium heat, sauté onion, bell pepper, celery, and garlic in margarine, until tender, about 10 minutes.
2. Add crawfish and fat. Cook until crawfish are done, about 15 minutes. Season well with salt and plenty of red pepper.
3. Add cheese. When melted, add onion tops and parsley.
4. Add breadcrumbs and adjust seasoning. Allow to cool.
5. Fill unbaked tart shells three-fourths full and pull sides of shell over top. Sides will not cover the entire top.
6. Bake at 350 degrees for approximately 20 minutes, until shell is golden brown.

Makes 16 pies.
– Shirley A. Pellerin

# OYSTER MUSHROOM PATTIES

**1 box frozen patty shells, (6 count) or 6 tart shells**
**1/4 cup butter or margarine**
**1/4 cup flour**
**1 medium onion, chopped**
**2 tbsp. finely chopped green onion**
**1 stalk celery, chopped fine**
**1 clove garlic, chopped fine**
**1/2 pint oysters**
**Salt and pepper, to taste**
**1 (4-oz.) can mushrooms**
**1/2 cup chopped parsley**

1. Bake patty shells as directed on package.
2. Sauté margarine and flour together, until golden.
3. Add onion, green onion, celery and garlic, stirring constantly for 2 to 3 minutes.
4. Add oysters, oyster liquid, salt and pepper and cook until thick.
5. Drain mushrooms, reserving juice; chop mushrooms.
6. Mix in mushrooms and parsley. If more liquid is needed, add a little of the mushroom liquid for the right consistency.
7. Remove the top and center of each baked patty shell; set aside.
8. Spoon the oyster mixture into each of the six shells.
9. Bake at 325 degrees for 20 to 30 minutes.
10. Replace top on each patty shell.

Makes six patties.
– Yvonne Verot Andersen
Contributed by Bonnie Walters Sarver

# OVEN-BAKED CRAB DIP

2 (8-oz.) packages cream
   cheese, softened
1 tbsp. Chablis or other dry
   white wine
1/2 tsp. mustard
1/4 tsp. salt
1/3 cup mayonnaise
1 tbsp. powdered sugar
1/2 tsp. onion juice
1/4 tsp. garlic salt
1/2 lb. white crabmeat
Chopped parsley
Crackers

1. Combine first 8 ingredients and mix well.
2. Gently stir in crabmeat.
3. Spoon crabmeat mixture into a lightly greased, 1-quart baking dish.
4. Bake at 375 degrees for 15 minutes.
5. Sprinkle with parsley.
6. Serve warm with crackers.
7. Makes about 3 cups of dip.
– Rosemary Abide Benitez
*The Best of South Louisiana Cooking*

# PEPPER JELLY

3 cups sugar
1 cup water
1/3 cup lemon juice
4 to 6 tbsp. hot sauce
1 (3-oz.) pouch liquid pectin
Red or green food coloring
Cream Cheese
Ritz Crackers

1. Bring sugar, water, lemon juice and hot sauce to a boil.
2. Add pectin, let come to a boil, then boil for one minute.
3. Add food coloring. Pour into jars.
4. Serve over cream cheese on Ritz crackers.
– Leslie Miller

# CRAB MORNAY

1 stick butter
4 tbsp. flour
1 pint half-and-half
1 tbsp. cooking sherry
1 cup grated cheese
1 lb. crabmeat, picked over for shells
   and cartilage
Salt, to taste
1 tsp. red pepper
Parsley and shallots, to liking

1. In a saucepan over medium heat, melt butter and blend in flour.
2. Add the rest of the ingredients one at a time. Cook for five minutes.
3. Delicious served warm in pastry shells or as a dip.
– Janice Beadle

# SHRIMP SALAD

2 lbs. boiled shrimp,
   peeled and deveined
2 hard-boiled eggs, chopped
1 stalk celery, chopped fine
1 small bell pepper, chopped fine
Few sprigs parsley, chopped fine

3 sweet pickles, chopped fine
1 bunch green onions, chopped fine
Salt, pepper and cayenne, to taste
Hot sauce, to taste
2 cups mayonnaise
Crisp lettuce

1. Cut shrimp into small pieces.
2. Add all remaining ingredients except lettuce, blending thoroughly.
3. Chill and serve on crisp lettuce.
– Jackie Manuel

# POTATO SALAD

8 large red potatoes, peeled
   and cut in chunks
8 hard-boiled eggs, chopped
Salt and pepper, to taste
2 cups mayonnaise
1/2 cup bread and butter
   pickles, finely chopped

1/2 cup green olives, finely
   chopped
1/4 cup chopped onion
1/4 cup chopped bell pepper
1/4 cup chopped celery

1. Bring a large pot of water to a boil. Add potatoes, and cook for 15
   minutes, or until tender but still firm. Drain and cool.
2. Place eggs in a saucepan and cover with cold water. Bring water to
   a boil and immediately remove from heat. Cover and let eggs
   stand in hot water for 15 minutes. Drain off hot water, rinse under
   cool water, peel and chop.
3. In a large bowl, combine chopped potatoes and eggs, salt and
   pepper. Mix together mayonnaise, pickles, olives, onion, bell
   pepper and celery.
Serves eight.
– Karen B. Pilgreen
Lafayette, La.

# PATÉ DE FOIS GRAS
## (LIVER PATÉ)

1 lb. chicken livers
1 lb. chicken gizzards
1/2 cup oil
1/2 cup flour

1 onion, chopped fine
6 cloves garlic, minced
1/2 cup water

1. Cook chicken livers and gizzards in boiling water until tender, about 45 minutes. Grind coarsely.
2. Make a roux by heating oil, adding flour, and cooking until well-browned, about 5 minutes, stirring constantly.
3. Add onion and garlic and fry until wilted.
4. Add livers and gizzards and cook about 15 minutes.
5. Add water and simmer slowly about 15 minutes.
6. Serve on toasted bread or in patty shells, with sherry wine.
– Madame Angelle Castillo Bulliard
Mistress, Old Castillo Hotel
St. Martinville, La.

# SHRIMP MOLD

1 lb. cooked shrimp
1 (10.75-oz.) can condensed
   tomato soup
1 (8-oz.) package cream cheese,
   softened
2 (.25-oz.) packets unflavored
   gelatin, softened in 1 cup water

1 cup finely chopped celery
1 cup finely chopped onion
1/2 cup minced green onion
1 cup mayonnaise
Worcestershire sauce, to taste
Red pepper, to taste

1. Drain shrimp; chop and mash with a fork.
2. Combine tomato soup and cream cheese in a medium saucepan over medium heat and mix well; pour gelatin into mixture and stir well.
3. In a large bowl, mix celery, onion, green onion, shrimp, and mayonnaise.
4. Add soup mixture, Worcestershire sauce, and red pepper and mix well.
5. Pour into a well-greased one-quart mold and chill overnight. Unmold onto a serving plate before serving. Serve with assorted crackers.
– Mary Laurent

## SHRIMP & OKRA GUMBO

Cliff, this recipe's author, was taught to make a gumbo stock first rather than jump right into making the gumbo. This extra step adds more flavor into the final gumbo.

**Gumbo stock (Recipe follows)**
**3 quarts water**
**1/2 cup roux**
**1/2 cup onion**
**1/2 cup bell pepper**
**1 tbsp. minced garlic**

**1 lb. sliced okra**
**3 tbsp. cooking oil**
**1 lb. peeled shrimp (reserve heads and peels)**
**1/2 cup green onion**

1. Make gumbo stock first.
2. Then add water, roux, onion, bell pepper and garlic to the stock and boil for 45 minutes to 1 hour.
3. While juice is boiling, sauté okra in oil for 10 minutes and set aside.
4. Add peeled shrimp and okra and cook for 20 minutes; season to taste.
5. Just before finished, add green onion.
6. Serve over hot rice.

### GUMBO STOCK

**3 quarts water**
**1/2 bell pepper**
**3 stalks celery**
**Heads and peels from 1 lb. shrimp**

**1 tbsp. Cajun seasoning**
**1 tbsp. minced garlic**
**1/4 large yellow onion**
**1/2 cup green onion**

1. Add stock ingredients above to a large stock pot and boil on medium-high heat for 45 minutes.
2. Strain juice into a large bowl, discard contents of pot and return gumbo stock to pot.

− Cliff & Amy Amox
Arnaudville, La.

# CRAWFISH & CORN SOUP

4 tsp. butter
1 onion, finely chopped
2 cloves garlic, minced
2 (12-oz.) cans evaporated skim milk
1 cup white wine or water

3 (10.5-oz.) cans golden corn soup or golden mushroom soup
1 (1-lb.) package frozen corn kernels
4 cups chicken broth or seafood stock
Salt and pepper, to taste
2 lbs. peeled crawfish tails
4 tsp. fresh chopped basil (or 1 tsp. dried)

1. Melt butter; add onion and sauté over medium heat until glossy and clear.
2. Add garlic and stir for a few minutes.
3. Add evaporated milk, wine, soup, corn, stock, and salt and pepper to taste. Cook for about 15 to 20 minutes, stirring frequently.
4. Add crawfish and cook over low heat until crawfish are tender, approximately 15 minutes.
5. Add basil and cook for about 10 minutes.

Serves eight to ten.
– Mary B. Landry

# CORN & POTATO SOUP

2 tbsp. butter
1/4 cup chopped green onion
1 tbsp. minced garlic
1 tsp. black pepper, or to taste
1 (3-oz.) package cream cheese

2 (10.5-oz.) cans condensed cream of potato soup, undiluted
1 (14.75-oz.) can cream-style corn
2 cups milk

1. Melt butter and sauté green onion, garlic, and pepper. Add cream cheese.
2. Once cream cheese is melted, add soup, corn and milk. Blend well and heat thoroughly.

Options: Add shrimp or crabmeat 10 minutes before serving and continue cooking until shrimp or crabmeat is done. Top with grated Cheddar cheese and bacon pieces.
Serves four.
– Kit Johnson

# CAJUN CORN SOUP

2 lbs. sirloin tip roast cut in 3/4-in. cubes and seasoned
1/2 cup cooking oil
2 yellow onions, chopped
1 bell pepper, chopped
3 stalks celery, chopped
3 cloves garlic, minced
2 (14-oz.) cans tomatoes, okra, and corn (drained)
2 (14-oz.) cans chicken broth
1 (14-oz.) can fire roasted tomatoes with garlic
2 packages frozen corn (half cobs) with corn stripped from the cob
2 cups water
2 tsp. Cajun seasoning

1. Brown meat in oil. As liquid accumulates from browning the meat, remove liquid and reserve it.
2. Once meat is well browned, return accumulated water to pot and add all remaining ingredients except corn. Cook over medium heat for 1 to 1 1/2 hours.
3. Add corn and cook for 15 minutes more.

− Cliff & Amy Amox
Arnaudville, La.

# ANDOUILLE & ARTICHOKE BISQUE

1/2 stick butter
1 large onion, chopped fine
1 each red bell pepper, yellow bell pepper, and green bell pepper, chopped fine
1 lb. andouille sausage, diced
3 tbsp. flour
1 cup dry vermouth
1 cup chicken broth
1 cup half-and-half
2 cups heavy whipping cream
1/4 tsp. cayenne pepper
1/4 tsp. black pepper
1 tbsp. basil
1/2 tbsp. oregano
1 cup shredded jalapeno cheese
2 cups quartered artichoke hearts
Salt to taste

1. Melt butter in a large pot. Sauté onion, peppers and andouille until the vegetables are tender and the sausage lightly browned.
2. Add flour. Cook 5 to 8 eight minutes until a blond roux forms.
3. Stir in remaining ingredients and cook until thickened.
Serves 10.

− Robin Trahan
Gold Medal *1995 Le Petite Classique*

# SEAFOOD GUMBO

1/2 cup flour
1/2 cup bacon drippings
2 cloves garlic, finely minced
2 cups chopped celery
2 cups chopped onion
6 cups chicken stock
6 cups hot water
Salt, black, and red pepper, to taste

6 to 8 gumbo crabs, cleaned, optional
3 lbs. raw shrimp, peeled and deveined
1 lb. fresh lump crabmeat, picked over for shells and cartilage
2 pints oysters with juice
Hot, cooked rice
1 cup chopped green onion tops

1. In a heavy iron pot, make a roux of flour and bacon drippings. Cook over medium heat, stirring constantly, until a rich brown color.
2. Add garlic, celery, and onion. Cook over low heat until vegetables are wilted.
3. Add chicken stock and hot water. Season to taste with salt, black and red pepper.
4. Bring to a boil and then add the pre-cooked gumbo crabs. Turn down the heat and simmer slowly, about 1 hour. Remove the gumbo crabs.
5. Add the shrimp and crabmeat. Simmer slowly about 20 minutes.
6. Add the oysters with juice and cook about 10 to 15 minutes longer.
7. Serve over rice. Sprinkle green onion tops over each serving.
Serves ten to 12.
− Connie Monies Gremillion
Lafayette, La.

# CREAM OF CELERY & CRAWFISH SOUP

3 stalks celery, chopped
1/2 stick butter
White Sauce (Recipe
follows)

2 cups half-and-half
1 lb. peeled crawfish tails
1 cup milk
Salt, pepper and paprika to taste

1. Prepare White Sauce.
2. Sauté chopped celery in butter for 3 minutes; do not over cook. Add White Sauce and stir until mixture is creamy.
3. Gradually add half-and-half and continue to stir; mixture will thicken as it cooks.
4. Stir in crawfish tails; slowly add milk to desired consistency.
5. Season with salt, pepper and paprika to taste.
6. Cover and turn off heat; let set until flavors mix.

## WHITE SAUCE

1/2 stick butter
3 tbsp. flour

1 cup half-and-half
Salt and pepper, to taste

1.  Melt butter on low heat and add flour, stirring constantly.
2. Gradually add half-and-half, stirring constantly.
3. Season and set aside.
Serves four.
– Donna R. Robinson

# WILD DUCK & OYSTER GUMBO

1 cup cooking oil
1 cup flour
1 large onion, chopped
2 wild ducks, cut in serving pieces
Salt, red pepper and black pepper
2 quarts warm water

2 tbsp. hot sauce
1 pint oysters
Parsley, minced
Green onion tops, minced
Filé powder, optional
Hot, cooked rice

1. Make a roux by combining oil and flour in a large heavy pot over medium-high heat; cook and stir until the flour browns, about 5 minutes.
2. Add onion and cook several minutes longer, stirring constantly.
3. Season ducks well with salt and pepper, then cook in roux until oil separates out around edges.
4. Add warm water, and cook slowly about 2 hours, until the ducks are tender.
5. Add hot sauce, salt and pepper to taste.
6. Add oysters about 20 minutes before serving.
7. Sprinkle with parsley and onion tops; add filé powder if desired.
8. Serve over cooked rice.

– Mrs. Melba Jean Patin
*Granny's Cajun Cookin'*

# CHICKEN & SAUSAGE GUMBO

1/2 cup finely chopped bell pepper
1 onion, chopped fine
1/2 cup chopped celery
1/4 cup cooking oil
2 tbsp. tomato paste
1 1/2 cups roux
3 1/2 cups boiling water
1 chicken, cut up

2 lbs. sausage cut into 2-inch lengths
1/4 cup chopped parsley
1/2 cup chopped green onion tops
Bootsie's Seasoning Salt
2 tsp. garlic powder
1 tsp. red pepper
Hot, cooked rice

1. Sauté bell pepper, onion and celery in cooking oil.
2. Add tomato paste, and cook for 20 minutes.

3. Dissolve roux in boiling water in a Dutch oven. Add sautéed vegetables to roux mixture and cook for 1 hour.
4. Add chicken, and cook 45 minutes longer.
5. Add sausage, and cook another 30 minutes.
6. Add parsley, green onions and seasonings.
7. Serve hot over rice.
– Bootsie John Landry
*The Best of South Louisiana Cooking*

# TURTLE SOUP

3 lbs. turtle meat
4 quarts water
1/2 cup shortening or oil
1/2 cup flour
3 stalks celery, chopped fine
1 large onion, chopped fine
6 pods garlic, chopped fine
1 large bell pepper, chopped fine

2 lemons, sliced thin
4 tbsp. Worcestershire sauce
Salt and pepper, to taste
3 heaping tbsp. Whole Spice, tied in a thin cloth
2/3 cup sherry
4 hard-boiled eggs
Parsley

1. Boil turtle meat in water until tender, about one hour. Skim to remove film.
2. Remove meat from stock and de-bone. Strain stock and set aside.
3. In a separate pot, make the roux by melting shortening over medium heat and slowly add flour, stirring constantly, until flour dissolves, and roux is a rich brown color.
4. Add celery, onion, garlic, and bell pepper to the roux and cook slowly until vegetables are wilted.
5. Add the reserved stock and turtle meat, and then lemons, Worcestershire sauce, salt and pepper.
6. Add the bag of spices and simmer for 1 hour.
7. Shortly before serving, add sherry.
8. Garnish each serving with sliced hard-boiled egg and parsley.
Serves 10 to 12.
– Linden Bercegeay

# CRAWFISH BISQUE

## PREPARATION

**50 lbs. live crawfish**

1. Rinse crawfish thoroughly. (See the Preparation process in the Cajun Crawfish Boil recipe on page 50 for how to clean crawfish.)
2. Steam crawfish in a large, deep container until shells are bright red. Do not over cook as this makes peeling difficult.
3. Plunge crawfish in cold water and begin peeling tails immediately.
4. Place crawfish tails in one bowl and fat in another. There should be about 10 pounds of tail meat.
5. Keep 100 shells (backs) for stuffing: Separate the crawfish head from the back; discard the head and remove the insides from the crawfish back and discard. Rinse out the empty backs and set aside for Stuffing.
6. Divide tail meat in half, and divide fat in half, and place in separate bowls; set aside.

## STUFFING FOR CRAWFISH BACKS

**1/2 cup oil**
**1/2 cup flour**
**2 large onions, chopped fine**
**8 cloves garlic, minced**
**1/2 reserved crawfish tails, ground fine**

**1/2 reserved crawfish fat**
**1 cup water**
**8 slices bread, toasted**
**Cayenne, black pepper and salt, to taste**
**100 prepared crawfish shells (backs)**

1. Heat oil in a large pot. Stir in flour and cook until roux is dark brown, stirring often. (Do not use a black iron pot; it will cause the crawfish to darken.)
2. Add onions and garlic and cook until wilted.
3. Add ground crawfish tails, crawfish fat and water.
4. Dip toasted bread in additional water and add to mixture, stirring to break up bread. Season with cayenne, black pepper and salt.
5. Cook mixture over medium heat about 15 minutes; remove from heat and cool.
6. Stuff backs with mixture and place in rows in a baking pan.
7. Bake 15 minutes in a 350-degree oven.

## BISQUE

3/4 cup cooking oil
3/4 cup flour
1 onion, chopped
3 cloves garlic, minced
1/2 reserved crawfish fat

1/2 reserved crawfish tails
6 cups water
Cayenne, black pepper and salt
Stuffed crawfish backs
Hot, cooked rice

1. Repeat Step 1 under Stuffing.
2. Add chopped onion and garlic, remaining crawfish fat, remaining crawfish tails and water. Add some of the stuffing to thicken gravy.
3. Simmer about 15 minutes. Season highly with cayenne, black pepper and salt.
4. Pour bisque into a deep bowl over stuffed backs. Serve over rice.
– de Della Guerin Wadlington
Contributed by Michelle Lemoine, LSU AgCenter
Evangeline Parish

# BOUILLABAISSE

1 cup cooking oil
6 lbs. gaspergou or red
   snapper, cut in chunks
2 tsp. salt
1 tsp. red pepper
2 onions, minced fine

2 cloves garlic, minced fine
1 small, sweet green pepper,
   minced fine
1 (28-oz.) can whole tomatoes,
   crushed

1. Choose a large, heavy pot, preferably iron or cast aluminum; grease the bottom and sides of pot thoroughly with oil.
2. Put a layer of well-seasoned fish at the bottom.
3. Spread generously with a layer of chopped vegetables and tomato.
4. Then add another layer of fish, another layer of chopped vegetables and tomato, and continue until all the fish has been put into the pot, ending with a layer of vegetables and tomatoes. Cover.
5. Cook over low heat for 2 hours or more, depending on the quantity. Do not stir, but shake the pot to prevent sticking.

This is a delicious French dish.
Serve with French bread or garlic bread.
– Contributed by Michelle Lemoine, LSU AgCenter
Evangeline Parish

# SHRIMP BISQUE

2 cups chopped celery
2 cups chopped yellow onion
1 1/2 bell pepper
2 tbsp. garlic
1 tbsp. Cajun seasoning
1/4 tsp. thyme

2 bay leaves
3 tbsp. butter
1 lb. peeled shrimp, reserve heads
   and peels for stock
Shrimp stock (Recipe follows)
Roux (Recipe follows)

1. Sauté celery, onion, bell pepper, garlic, seasoning, thyme and bay leaves in butter for 15 minutes until onion turns clear.
2. Add shrimp, cook 6 minutes.
3. Add stock and bring to a boil.
4. Slowly add the roux, stirring constantly until dissolved.
5. Reduce heat to low and simmer 15-20 minutes.
6. Remove bay leaves, and puree bisque in blender.
Serve immediately.

## STOCK

3 quarts water
1/2 bell pepper
3 stalks celery
Shrimp heads and peels

1 tbsp. seasoning
1 tbsp. minced garlic
1/4 large yellow onion

1. Add all ingredients to stock pot; boil on medium-high heat for 45 minutes.
2. Strain juice into another pot or bowl and set aside.

## ROUX

1 cup cooking oil

1 1/4 cup flour

1. In a cast iron Dutch oven or skillet, add oil and flour together, stirring continuously. Cook for 1 hour 15 minutes over low heat, stirring continuously, until dark brown.
2. After cooking, set aside in small bowl.
– Cliff & Amy Amox
Arnaudville, La.

# CHICKEN, SAUSAGE & OKRA GUMBO

Gumbo stock (Recipe follows)
3 cups fresh or frozen okra
3 tbsp. cooking oil
2 links fresh pork sausage, sliced
2 links homemade smoked
  sausage, sliced

1 (3-lb.) fryer, cut up, reserve
  chicken back
2 onions, chopped
1 bell pepper, chopped
3 stalks celery, chopped
3 cloves garlic, minced
Parsley, to taste

1. Get gumbo stock cooking.
2. In a Dutch oven, sauté okra in oil over medium heat for 10 minutes or until no longer sticky. Remove and set aside.
3. Brown all sausage in Dutch oven 15 minutes, remove and set aside.
4. Season chicken and brown in Dutch oven over medium heat for 15 minutes or until medium brown; then remove, de-bone and set aside.
5. Sauté vegetables in Dutch oven until wilted.
6. After removing the chicken back from pot, add okra, sausage, chicken and vegetables to pot. Slightly reduce heat and boil for 1 to 1 1/2 hours, seasoning to taste with Cajun seasoning or salt, pepper, and red pepper.

NOTE: For intact okra, add 20 minutes before finished; for broken okra, add sooner.

## GUMBO STOCK

6 quarts water
Chicken back
1 cup roux

1. In a 12-quart stock pot bring water to a boil over high heat.
2. Separate the chicken back from fryer and place in pot.
3. Once water is boiling, add roux and stir to dissolve. Boil for 30 minutes, then remove chicken back.

– Cliff & Amy Amox
Arnaudville, La.

## MEAT, POULTRY & WILD GAME

## ANDOUILLE SAUSAGE

Andouille (pronounced "ahn-DOO-wee") is a Cajun smoked sausage that is nationally famous today. The andouille is slowly smoked over pecan wood and sugar cane. When smoked, it becomes very dark to almost black in color.

| | |
|---|---|
| 5 lbs. pork butt | 1/2 cup chopped garlic |
| 1/2 lb. pork fat | 1/4 cup cracked black pepper |
| 1 tbsp. dry thyme | 2 tbsp. cayenne pepper |
| 4 tbsp. salt | 6 feet of beef middle casing (see butcher or specialty shop) |

1. Cube pork butt into 1 1/2 -inch cubes.
2. Using a meat grinder with four 1/4-inch holes in the grinding plate, grind pork and pork fat. (If you do not have a grinding plate this size, I suggest hand cutting pork butt into 1/4-inch-square pieces.)
3. Place ground pork in a large mixing bowl, and blend in all remaining ingredients except casing.
4. Once well blended, stuff meat into casings in 1-foot links, using the sausage attachment on your meat grinder.
5. Tie both ends of the sausage securely using a heavy gauge twine.
6. In your home-style smoker, smoke andouille at 175 to 200 degrees, for approximately 4 to 5 hours using pecan or hickory wood.
7. The andouille may then be frozen, and used for seasoning gumbos, white or red beans, pastas or grilling as an hors d'oeuvre.

– Chef John Folse
Gonzales, La.
Contributed by Charley & Ruth Addison,
*Cooking With Crazy Charley Part 3*

# ALLIGATOR SAUCE PIQUANTE

2 small onions, chopped
4 tbsp. butter
1 (6-oz.) can tomato paste
1/2 tsp. sugar
1/2 cup chopped bell pepper
1/2 cup chopped celery
4 cloves garlic, chopped
1 (8-oz.) can mushrooms,
    stems and pieces

3 cups water
1/4 cup chopped parsley
4 lbs. alligator meat, cut into
    small pieces
Salt and black pepper, to taste
Cayenne pepper, to taste
1 small jar olives
Hot, cooked rice

1. Sauté onions in butter until brown.
2. Add tomato paste and sugar and cook about 5 minutes.
3. Stir in bell pepper, celery, garlic, mushrooms and cook 5 minutes.
4. Add water and cook 1 hour over low heat.
5. Add parsley, alligator (preferably meat other than from the tail), salt, pepper, and cayenne.
6. Cover pot and cook slowly for 45 minutes or until meat is tender.
7. Add olives that have been soaked in water and cook for a few minutes longer.
8. Serve over rice.
– Jackie Manuel

# CAJUN MEAT MARINADE

1 quart cooking oil
1 bottle Worcestershire sauce
4 tbsp. dry mustard
2 tbsp. garlic juice

1/2 (16-oz.) bottle vinegar
1 (8-oz.) can tomato sauce
1 (24-oz.) bottle ketchup
Seasoning, to taste

Mix all ingredients and cook 15 minutes and cool before using on meat.
– Mrs. Hugh Miller

# BAKED CHICKEN

| | |
|---|---|
| 4 fryers, split in half | Lemon pepper seasoning |
| Garlic powder | Chili powder |
| Salt | 2 cups chicken broth |
| Red pepper | Paprika |
| Black pepper | Parsley flakes |

1. Season the fryer halves well by rubbing garlic powder, salt, peppers, and chili powder into both sides. Place fryers in baking pans.
2. Preheat oven to 275 degrees.
3. Pour chicken broth over fryers and sprinkle with paprika and parsley flakes.
4. Cook for three to five hours, basting about every half hour until very dark brown.

The slow cooking and basting process makes this a very delicious, rich-tasting main dish.
  – Junior Lagneaux, Lagneaux's Restaurant
Lafayette, La.

# SQUIRREL FRICASSÉE

| | |
|---|---|
| 3 or 4 squirrels | 2 tbsp. butter |
| Herb Flour (Recipe follows) | 3/4 cup sherry |

1. Clean squirrels, wash well and cut in serving pieces.
2. Put Herb Flour in a clean paper bag; add squirrel, a few pieces at a time, and shake until thoroughly coated.
3. Heat butter in a heavy iron skillet or Dutch oven; add squirrel and cook until browned on all sides.
4. Pour off some of the fat and add sherry wine; cover and simmer for 1 hour.
5. Make a sauce with what is left of the liquid in the pan, thickening with a little of the flour, if desired.

## HERB FLOUR

**1 cup flour**
**1/2 tsp. freshly ground black pepper**
**1 tbsp. powdered marjoram**
**1 tbsp. salt**
**1/2 tsp. allspice**
– Mrs. Melba Jean Patin
*Granny's Cajun Cookin'*

# BAKED WILD DUCK OR GOOSE

*MARINADE*
**Cooking oil**
**Vinegar**
**Chopped onion**
**Garlic**
**Salt and pepper**

**2 wild ducks or geese**
**2 raw turnips**
**1/4 cup cooking oil**
**1/2 cup water**
**1 cup chopped onion**
**1 cup chopped bell pepper**
**1 (4-oz.) can whole mushrooms**
**Salt and pepper, to taste**

1. Combine enough cooking oil, vinegar, onion, garlic, salt and pepper to marinate duck.
2. Place birds in marinade; cover and marinate in refrigerator for 24 hours.
3. Remove birds from marinade. Stuff each wing, breast, thigh and leg with half a clove of garlic, and place a whole turnip in cavity of each bird.
4. Heat the 1/4-cup oil in a heavy pot over medium heat. Brown birds in oil on all sides.
5. Add all remaining ingredients to pot and bring to a simmer. Cover, reduce heat to low, and simmer until birds are tender, 2 to 2 1/2 hours.

Makes eight servings.
– Junior Lagneaux, Lagneaux's Restaurant
Lafayette

# OLD-FASHIONED TOMATO GRAVY

1 1/2 lbs. bacon, diced
1 onion, chopped
2 tbsp. flour

Salt and pepper, to taste
1 (14 1/4-oz.) can diced tomatoes
3 cups tomato juice

1. In a skillet, cook bacon until crisp. Drain all but 2 tablespoons of the drippings.
2. Cook onion in drippings until tender.
3. Stir in flour, salt and pepper; cook and stir over low heat until mixture is golden.
4. Add tomatoes and tomato juice. Stir well.
5. Bring to a boil for 2 minutes. Reduce heat and simmer uncovered for 15 minutes or until thickened. Stir in bacon. Serve over corn bread.
– Sandra Baglo

# RABBIT SAUCE PIQUANTE

3 tbsp. flour
5 tbsp. cooking oil
4 large onions, chopped
1 clove garlic, chopped fine
1 cup chopped parsley stems
3 cups canned tomatoes

1 (3-lb.) rabbit, cut into pieces
Water
1 cup chopped green onion
1/4 cup chopped parsley leaves
Red pepper and salt, to taste
Hot, cooked rice

1. Brown the flour in oil to make a roux.
2. Add onions, garlic, and parsley stems, and cook until tender.
3. Add tomatoes and cook until well blended.
4. In another skillet brown rabbit pieces quickly in a little oil; add to tomato mixture.
5. Add water to make gravy of desired consistency; cover and cook slowly until rabbit is tender.
6. Add green onions and parsley leaves; adjust seasonings.
7. Serve with rice.
– Mrs. Melba Jean Patin
*Granny's Cajun Cookin'*

# RED BEANS & RICE

1 lb. dried red beans
Water
1 lb. smoked pork sausage,
    sliced
1 onion, chopped
1/2 bell pepper, chopped

Green onion tops
1 bay leaf
1 clove garlic, minced
Salt and pepper, to taste
2 tbsp. Worcestershire sauce
1/4 cup milk, optional
Hot, cooked rice

1. Sort and rinse beans; cover with water and soak overnight.
2. Brown the sausage, and then remove from pot.
3. In the sausage drippings, sauté onion, bell pepper and onion tops until tender.
4. Return sausage to pot; add beans and enough water to cover them and bring to a boil.
5. Add bay leaf, garlic, salt and pepper. Cook for 1 to 1 1/2 hours.
6. Add Worcestershire sauce and continue cooking until creamy, one-half to one hour. Taste and add more salt if desired.
7. If you prefer thicker beans, add milk. Cook until desired consistency.
8. Serve over rice.
  – Junior Lagneaux, Lagneaux's Restaurant
Lafayette

# CHICKEN SAUCE PIQUANTE

1 fryer, cut in pieces
3 tbsp. cooking oil
1 onion, chopped
1 bell pepper, chopped

Parsley flakes
2 (8-oz.) cans tomato sauce
1 cup water
Salt and pepper, to taste
Hot, cooked rice

1. Brown chicken in oil; remove from pot and brown onion and bell pepper.
2. Add chicken, parsley flakes, tomato sauce, water and seasonings and mix well; simmer about 40 minutes.
3. Serve over rice.
  – Joey Jenkins

# CHICKEN & SAUSAGE JAMBALAYA

9 chicken thighs
1 lb. smoked sausage, sliced
3 medium onions, chopped
4 stalks celery, chopped
2 bell peppers, chopped
5 cloves garlic, chopped
Olive oil
1 (28-oz.) can tomatoes

1 (6-oz.) can tomato paste
Cayenne pepper
Chili powder
Parsley flakes
Worcestershire sauce
Hot sauce
Salt and pepper
1 cup uncooked rice

1. Boil chicken and sausage until tender; reserve broth.
2. Sauté chopped onions, celery, bell peppers, and garlic in olive oil.
3. Add chicken, sausage, tomatoes and tomato paste.
4. Add seasoning to taste and cook 30-45 minutes on low heat.
5. Add 2 to 2 1/2 cups of reserved broth and rice. Cover and cook until rice is tender.

Serves about eight.
– Florence Gauthier


# BARBECUED ALLIGATOR

2 lbs. alligator fillets
Vinegar
4 to 5 tsp. prepared mustard

Salt and pepper, to taste
Barbeque sauce

1. Sprinkle alligator fillets with vinegar, roll in mustard, and season with salt and pepper. Let stand for 1 hour.
2. Barbeque on low fire without basting for about 1 hour.
3. Butterfly fillets by slicing almost in half and placing the outside down. Baste inside with your favorite barbeque sauce and cook until done.

– Jackie Manuel

# CHICKEN FRICASSÉE

1/2 cup oil
1/2 cup flour
1 medium yellow onion, chopped
1 bell pepper, chopped

3 cloves garlic, minced
Water
1 fryer, cut up
Salt and pepper, to taste
Hot sauce, to taste

1. In a Dutch oven over medium heat, combine oil and flour and stir until roux is dark brown.
2. Add onion, bell pepper and garlic and sauté until limp.
3. Fill pot two-thirds full of water. Add chicken and seasonings and bring to a boil.
4. Reduce heat to medium and cook 1 hour or until chicken is done.

# BLACK-EYED PEA & SAUSAGE JAMBALAYA IN RICE COOKER

1 lb. smoked sausage, sliced
1/2 stick butter or margarine
1 1/4 cups (10-oz.) raw rice
1 (15.5-oz.) can black-eyed peas with jalapenos
1 (10.5-oz.) can beef broth

1 onion, chopped
1 bell pepper, chopped
3 cloves garlic, minced
1/2 cup chopped green onion
Chopped parsley

1. For the best flavor, brown the sausage in skillet and drain excess grease.
2. Add all ingredients to rice cooker, stir, cover and press down COOK switch.
3. Once meal is cooked, and the COOK switch pops up to WARM mode, let it stand covered 10 minutes before serving.
Serves five or six.
– From *Rice Cooker Meals: Fast Home Cooking for Busy People*, by Neal Bertrand
Lafayette, La.

# HOW TO MAKE A ROUX

A roux (pronounced roo) is a mixture of oil and flour, which is used to thicken soups and gravies. It is considered one of the basic techniques which good Cajun cooks learn at an early age.

**1 cup cooking oil**
**1 cup all-purpose flour**

1. Heat the oil in a heavy pot over medium heat. A black iron skillet is best. When the oil is hot, gradually stir in the flour. Stir constantly or the flour will burn.
2. Lower heat as soon as all the flour has been added. Continue to stir the mixture with a slow, even motion.
3. After all of the flour has dissolved in the oil, turn the heat down to very low and cook until roux is a deep, golden brown color, stirring constantly. This may take as long as 30 minutes.
4. Once the roux is a deep, golden brown, remove from the pot and set aside. If the roux remains in the pot it will continue to cook and get too dark. It is now ready to use.
5. Make extra roux to keep for use later. It stores well in the refrigerator. Always use warm water to dissolve roux.

**Tips on using roux:**
• The roux may be added by the spoonful to a liquid, such as a soup or gumbo, to thicken. Stir well to dissolve the roux and thicken the liquid.
• Vegetables such as onion and celery may be added to the almost-done roux and allowed to cook, slowly, until the vegetables are wilted and the roux is golden brown.
• Stir a little liquid into the vegetable-roux mixture and then add to the soup or gumbo. This allows the liquid to accept the roux better.
• When making a roux for a gumbo, be sure to skim off any excess oil that is not absorbed by the flour. If you don't, the excess oil will make the gumbo too rich.

# EGGPLANT & BEEF CASSEROLE

1 medium eggplant, peeled
   and cubed
1 lb. ground meat
1/4 cup chopped onion
1/4 cup chopped bell pepper
1 (10.75-oz.) can condensed
   cream of mushroom soup

1 egg, beaten
1/2 cup evaporated milk
1 cup grated sharp cheese
3/4 cup bread stuffing mix
Topping for casserole (Recipe
   follows)

1. Boil eggplant in salted water; drain and mash.
2. Brown meat with onion and pepper until tender.
3. Mix remaining ingredients except Topping with meat mixture.
4. Add mashed eggplant and mix well.
5. Place in a greased casserole dish and sprinkle Topping over top.
6. Bake for 25 minutes at 350 degrees.

## *TOPPING*

2 tbsp. melted butter or margarine
1/2 cup stuffing mix
1 cup grated sharp cheese

Mix all ingredients in a bowl and sprinkle over casserole.
− Merline Morvant

# ROUND STEAK & GRAVY

1/2 stick butter
1 medium onion, chopped fine
1 medium bell pepper,
  chopped fine
4 large cloves garlic,
  chopped fine

2 lbs. round steak, trimmed of
  excess fat
Salt and red pepper, to taste
2 cups water
Hot, cooked rice

1. Melt butter in a black iron Dutch oven, over medium heat. Add onion, bell pepper and garlic and cook until wilted; remove from pot and reserve.
2. Cut steak in hand-sized pieces. Season both sides with salt and pepper and rub in.
3. Brown steak thoroughly on both sides in remaining butter, adding more butter if needed. Add a little water if needed to prevent burning.
4. Add water and the sautéed vegetables; cover and cook over medium-low heat until steak is tender, about 30 to 45 minutes, adding more water if more gravy is needed.
5. Serve over rice.
Serves four.
– Neal Bertrand
Lafayette, La.

# SLOW COOKER BEEF ROAST

1 (2 to 3-lb.) beef roast, cut in half
5 medium potatoes, cut in cubes
1/2 (1-lb.) bag frozen baby carrots
2 cups cherry tomatoes
1/2 cup chopped celery
1/2 cup chopped bell pepper

1 onion, chopped
Dash Worcestershire sauce
1 tbsp. mustard
Salt and pepper, to taste
1 tbsp. parsley flakes

1. Put all ingredients in slow cooker and top with seasonings.
2. Cook on low heat for 8 to 10 hours or until meat is tender.
3. Serve over rice.
– Trisha Ardoin

# SLOW COOKER BEEF BRISKET

1 cup ketchup
1/4 cup grape jelly
1 package dry onion soup

1/2 tsp. black pepper
1 (3 to 3 1/2-lb.) fresh beef
   brisket, cut in half

1. Combine ketchup, jelly, onion soup, and pepper and mix well.
2. Place half of the beef in slow cooker and cover with half of sauce.
3. Add remaining beef and cover with remaining sauce.
4. Cover and cook on low for 8 to 10 hours or until meat is tender.
5. Slice and serve with sauce.
– Mrs. Ola Devilbiss
Contributed by Dorothy McCarty


# VENISON STEW WITH DUMPLINGS

2 lbs. venison meat, cut into cubes
1 tsp. salt
1/4 tsp. pepper
3 tbsp. flour
Cooking oil or shortening
Boiling water
1 cup diced carrots

1 cup diced turnips
1 cup tiny onions
3 cups cubed potatoes
1/4 tsp. garlic powder
Dumplings

1. Season meat with salt and pepper, then roll in flour.
2. Brown meat in oil in a large black pot over medium heat.
3. Cover meat with boiling water and simmer until tender.
4. Add carrots, turnips and onions; simmer for 30 minutes longer.
5. Add potatoes and garlic powder; simmer for another 30 minutes.
6. Add favorite dumpling recipe about 15 minutes before serving
   time, cover and do not uncover until done.
– Mrs. Melba Jean Patin
*Granny's Cajun Cookin'*

# TONY'S OLD-FASHIONED CHICKEN STEW

1 fat hen or rooster (about 6
   lbs.), cut up
Tony's Creole Seasoning, or
   salt and pepper
1 stick butter or margarine
3/4 cup milk
1/2 cup flour

1 onion, chopped fine
2 stalks celery, chopped
1 green bell pepper, chopped
3 cloves garlic, chopped fine
Water
1 tbsp. Worcestershire sauce
Hot, cooked rice or spaghetti

1. Season hen with Creole seasoning or salt and pepper.
2. Melt butter in a Dutch oven.
3. Dip chicken in milk, and then flour; fry in butter until brown; remove chicken.
4. Sauté onion, celery, bell pepper and garlic in drippings until tender.
5. Add chicken, Worcestershire sauce and enough water to cover; cover the pot and cook slowly until hen is tender, about 4 hours.
6. Serve over rice or spaghetti.

Serves eight.

– Tony Chachere
*Tony Chachere's Cajun Country Cookbook*

# SQUIRREL STEW

8 to 10 squirrels, cleaned and
   cut up
Salt and pepper, to taste
2 1/2 cups flour
2 cups vegetable oil
2 bell peppers, finely chopped
4 onions, finely chopped
Half bunch celery, finely
   chopped
1 bunch parsley, finely chopped

2 bunches green onions, finely
   chopped
8 cloves garlic, finely chopped
Water
Kitchen Bouquet
8 or 10 chicken or beef bouillon
   cubes
Hot sauce
Red pepper
Hot, cooked rice

1. Season squirrels with salt and pepper and shake in paper bag with enough flour to coat squirrel well.
2. In a large pot heat vegetable oil and fry squirrel until lightly browned.
3. Remove squirrel to another container and hold in warm oven while making roux.

4. Stir flour remaining in bag into pot; cook until it makes a brown roux, stirring often.
5. Add vegetables and squirrels and cover with water.
6. Add enough Kitchen Bouquet to give stew a nice brown color and the bouillon cubes.
7. Season to taste with salt, pepper, hot sauce and red pepper if desired.
8. Stir well and bring to a boil. Lower heat to simmer and cook for about five hours.
9. Serve over rice along with a tossed green salad and hot French bread.
Serves about 15.

# SMOTHERED CHICKEN

1 chicken, cut into pieces
Salt, pepper, and other
   seasonings, to taste
1/4 cup oil
5 tsp. sugar
Water

3 large onions, chopped
1 large bell pepper, chopped
3 tbsp. flour
1/2 cup chopped green onion
1/2 cup chopped parsley
Hot, cooked rice or potatoes

1. Season chicken.
2. In heavy pot, over medium heat, heat oil until hot.
3. Add sugar and stir until medium brown in color.
4. Add chicken and brown on all sides. Continue cooking until chicken is done, about 45 minutes, adding small amounts of water as chicken cooks to keep drippings from burning.
5. Add onions and bell pepper. Cook for 15 more minutes, then remove chicken from pot.
6. Dissolve flour in some water and gradually stir into gravy; cook and stir until thickened to desired consistency, adding more water if needed.
7. Add green onion and parsley just before serving.
8. Serve over rice or potatoes.
Baked Variation: Once chicken is browned, add remaining ingredients and bake at 350 degrees for one hour or until done.
Serves four to six.
– Gene Lognion, Blue Ribbon Chef
Lafayette

# SMOTHERED SQUIRREL

3 or 4 cleaned squirrels, cut
   into serving pieces
Salt and pepper, to taste
Cooking oil
1 large bell pepper, chopped
1 stalk celery, chopped

1 large onion, chopped
4 cloves garlic, minced
Water
1 (4-oz.) can sliced mushrooms,
   undrained
Hot, cooked rice

1. Season squirrel with salt and pepper.
2. Add enough cooking oil in heavy black pot to cover bottom, plus two tablespoons extra.
3. Brown squirrel pieces well, until all water has been absorbed and meat starts to shrink off the bones.
4. Add bell pepper, celery, onion and garlic and smother down until all is wilted.
5. Add enough water to cover squirrel, and cook over low heat until squirrel is tender.
6. Stir in mushrooms and cook 10 minutes longer.
7. Serve with rice and black-eyed peas.
– Darrell Patin
*Granny's Cajun Cookin'*

# SMOTHERED VEAL LIVER

1 1/2 lbs. fresh veal liver
Salt and black pepper, to taste
1/2 tsp. red pepper, or to taste
1/2 cup cooking oil

2 large onions, diced
1 bell pepper, diced
1 cup water
Hot, cooked rice or grits

1. Cut liver into serving-size pieces; season with salt and peppers.
2. Add enough oil to a heavy skillet to cover the bottom.
3. When oil is hot, reduce heat; brown liver for 10 minutes on each side.
4. Remove liver from pot; add onions and bell pepper and sauté until wilted.
5. Add water and liver to pot and cook for no longer than 15 minutes.
6. Serve over rice or grits.
– Junior Lagneaux, Lagneaux's Restaurant
Lafayette, La.

# TASSO

Tasso, a highly seasoned, intensely flavored smoked pork, adds a wonderful flavor to a variety of dishes, from soups to jambalaya to pastas and seafood dishes.

| | |
|---|---|
| **8 to 10 lb. boneless pork butt** | **5 tbsp. cayenne pepper** |
| **2 tbsp. paprika** | **2 tbsp. garlic powder or** |
| **5 tbsp. salt** | **granulated garlic** |
| **1 tbsp. curing salt** | **3 tbsp. freshly ground black pepper** |
| **2 tbsp. cinnamon** | **3 tbsp. white pepper** |

1. Trim the pork of all excess fat and cut it into strips about 1-inch thick and at least 4 inches long.
2. Mix together the seasonings and place in a shallow pan. Roll each strip of pork in the seasoning mixture and place on a tray. Cover with plastic wrap and refrigerate at least overnight (preferably two days).
3. Prepare your smoker. Place the pork strips on a grill or rod and smoke until done, 5 to 7 hours. Don't let the smoker get too hot.
4. Remove the meat and let it cool completely, then wrap well in plastic and foil.
5. The tasso will keep well in the refrigerator for up to 10 days, and it also freezes very well.

– Chef Alex Patout
Alex Patout's Louisiana Restaurant
New Orleans, La.
Contributed by Charley & Ruth Addison,
*Cooking With Crazy Charley Part 3*

# VENISON ROAST

1 (5- to 6-lb.) venison roast
Salt, red pepper and black
   pepper, to taste
Chopped garlic, onion, and
   bell pepper, to taste

Prepared mustard
Milk
Cooking oil
Water

1. Season the roast with salt and pepper.
2. In a bowl combine chopped garlic, onion and bell pepper,
   prepared mustard and salt and pepper; mix well.
3. Cut slits into roast, and stuff mixture inside.
4. Place roast in a large bowl and add enough milk to completely
   cover roast.
5. Cover and refrigerate for two or three days. (The longer it soaks in
   milk, the more tender the roast will be.)
6. Remove roast from milk and pat dry.
7. Heat oil in a large heavy pot over low heat; add roast and cook
   until very tender, adding small amounts of water occasionally as
   needed. Cooking time varies depending on size of roast.
– Mrs. Melba Jean Patin
*Granny's Cajun Cookin'*


# BARBECUE SAUCE

2 sticks butter
1 quart cooking oil
Juice of 1 large lemon
1 large onion, chopped

3 or 4 bay leaves
2 tbsp. Worcestershire sauce
1 tbsp. garlic powder
Salt and pepper, to taste

Mix all sauce ingredients together and simmer for 30 to 45 minutes.
– Palmer J. Bienvenu
Contributed by Ann Marie Hightower

# SEAFOOD

## BAKED FISH

6 to 8 lbs. catfish or red snapper
    fillets
Seasoning, to taste
2 sticks butter or margarine
2 cups chopped celery
2 cups chopped bell pepper
2 cups chopped onion
1/2 cup chopped parsley
1 clove garlic, minced
1/2 cup lemon juice
1/2 cup white wine

1. Season fish and place in a baking pan. Combine remaining
   ingredients, except wine and spoon on top of fish.
2. Bake, uncovered in 350-degree oven about 1 hour, basting often.
3. Add wine and baste again. Cook about 10 minutes longer.
− Diana Gotte

## BARBECUED SHRIMP

3 lbs. unpeeled jumbo shrimp,
    heads on
1 lb. butter
1 (5-oz.) bottle Worcestershire
    sauce
1 tsp. garlic powder
Coarse ground black pepper,
    to taste
1 tsp. onion salt
Hot sauce, to taste

1. Put shrimp in a baking dish.
2. Cut butter into cubes and layer on top of shrimp.
3. Add Worcestershire sauce, garlic powder, black pepper, onion salt
   and hot sauce.
4. Bake, uncovered, in a 350-degree oven for 30 to 45 minutes.
5. Serve with hot French bread.
Serves four to six.
− Monica R. Domingue

# CATFISH COURTBOUILLON

1/4 onion, chopped
1/4 bell pepper, chopped
1/4 stalk celery, chopped
1/2 tbsp. roux
1 quart water
2 (8-oz.) cans tomato sauce

1 (6-oz.) can tomato paste
1/2 (10-oz.) can tomatoes with
  green chilies
Creole seasoning, to taste
4 lbs. catfish fillets or other
  white-fleshed fish

1. Combine all ingredients except fish in a pot or Dutch oven over medium heat; season to taste, bring to a boil and cook 1 hour.
2. Add catfish to sauce and cook about 45 minutes, or until fish flakes easily with a fork.

NOTE: Never stir Catfish Courtbouillon. In order to keep the mixture from sticking, shake the pot.

Serves eight.
– Junior Lagneaux, Lagneaux's Restaurant
Lafayette

# CORN & OYSTER CASSEROLE

1/4 cup melted butter
1 1/2 cups cracker crumbs,
  divided
1/2 cup chopped onion
1/2 cup chopped celery
2 tbsp. butter
1 pint oysters with 1/2 cup
  oyster liquid

1 (16-oz.) can whole kernel corn,
  drained
1 (2-oz.) jar diced pimentos
1 tbsp. Worcestershire sauce
1/2 tsp. salt
Pepper, to taste

1. Combine melted butter and 1 cup of the cracker crumbs. Set aside.
2. Sauté onion and celery in butter.
3. Stir in the oyster liquid, corn, pimentos, Worcestershire sauce, and seasonings.
4. Place buttered cracker crumbs in a lightly greased 10 x 6 x 2-inch baking dish. Arrange oysters over crumbs.
5. Spoon vegetable mixture on top. Cover with remaining 1/2 cup of cracker crumbs.
6. Bake at 375 degrees for about 35 minutes or until golden brown.

Serves six.
– Marie LeJeune

# BOILED SHRIMP OR CRABS

2 lbs. shrimp or crabs
4 quarts water
1 cup chopped celery
3 tbsp. salt

3 green onions, chopped
1 (3-oz.) bag shrimp or crab boil
Juice of one lemon

1. Fill an 8-quart stockpot a little more than half full of cold water. Add all remaining ingredients except shrimp.
2. Bring water and seasoning to a boil; cover and simmer for 20 minutes, letting the full flavor of the seasonings mix with the water.
3. Turn off heat and let flavors marry for about 10 more minutes.
4. Bring mixture back to a rapid boil. Add shrimp, turn heat off, and let stand for 6 to 8 minutes.
5. For crab and lobster: After adding to the pot, cover and return to a boil. When steam starts escaping from under the lid, lower the heat and cook for 15 minutes. Turn off heat and let sit, covered, for 10 minutes more.
 Note: Shrimp have a vein that runs down their back, and on all shrimp of any size one must remove the vein before eating.
– Charley & Ruth Addison
*Cooking With Crazy Charley Part 3*


# FISH SAUCE

1/4 cup finely chopped onion
3/4 cup finely chopped
   bell pepper
1/4 stalk celery, chopped fine
1 (15-oz.) can tomato sauce

1/2 (10-oz.) can tomatoes with
   green chilies
1/4 tsp. Creole seasoning
2 cups water

1. Mix all ingredients together and bring to boil; cook for 1 hour.
2. Season to taste.
3. Pour over any white-fleshed fish.
Makes three pints of sauce.
– Junior Lagneaux
Lagneaux's Restaurant
Lafayette, La.

# CRAWFISH JAMBALAYA IN RICE COOKER

NOTE: Shrimp, fish or the meat of your choice may be substituted for crawfish.

1 lb. peeled crawfish tails
2 1/2 rice-cooker cups (15-oz.) uncooked rice
1 (10.5-oz.) can chicken broth
1 (8-oz.) can tomato sauce
1 (4-oz.) can mushroom pieces
1 jalapeno pepper, finely chopped
1 medium onion, chopped
1 medium bell pepper, chopped
1/2 stick butter, chopped
Cajun or Creole seasoning, to taste
2/3 cup (6 oz.) water

1. Add all ingredients to rice cooker, stir, cover and press down COOK switch.
2. Once meal is cooked, and the COOK switch pops up to WARM mode, let it stand covered 10 minutes before serving.

Cooked 29 minutes and made up to the 5-cup level.
– Contributed by Elsie Castille
Breaux Bridge, La.
Reprinted from *Rice Cooker Meals: Fast Home Cooking for Busy People* by Neal Bertrand.

# CRABMEAT OR CRAWFISH AU GRATIN

3 stalks celery, chopped fine
1 large onion, chopped fine
2 sticks butter
4 tbsp. flour
1 large can evaporated milk
2 egg yolks
1 lb. grated American or Cheddar cheese, divided
2 lbs. crabmeat or peeled crawfish tails
Salt and pepper, to taste

1. Sauté celery and onion in butter over medium heat until thoroughly cooked.
2. Add flour and milk.
3. Whisk in egg yolks, stirring constantly.
4. Add cheese slowly, stirring constantly. Reserve a small portion of cheese for topping.

5. Add crabmeat last. (If crawfish are used, chop one pound fine and add one pound whole.) Season to your taste.
6. Pour in baking dish. Top with remaining cheese.
7. Bake at 400 degrees until cheese is a little brown. Filling is really cooked before putting in oven.
– Beverly Klumpp

# SHRIMP CREOLE

1/2 cup chopped onion
1/4 cup chopped green onion
1/4 cup chopped bell pepper
1/4 cup chopped celery
2 tbsp. minced garlic
2 tbsp. butter or margarine
3/4 cup chopped mushrooms
2 tbsp. all-purpose flour
1 (10-oz.) can tomatoes with green chilies, chopped and drained
1 to 2 tbsp. tomato paste, optional
Fresh, peeled tomatoes, in amount desired
2 cups seafood stock or water
1 lb. small shrimp, peeled, deveined and seasoned
Worcestershire sauce, salt, red and black pepper, to taste
1 to 2 tbsp. cornstarch dissolved in water
Hot, cooked rice

1. In a large skillet over medium heat, sauté onion, green onion, bell pepper, celery and garlic in butter until clear, approximately 5 or 6 minutes; add mushrooms.
2. Add flour, stirring often and scraping bottom of pan, 5 or 6 minutes.
3. Add tomatoes, tomato paste and fresh tomatoes, if desired; simmer for several minutes longer.
4. Add seafood stock, cover and simmer over low heat for 20 minutes; season to taste.
5. Season shrimp with Worcestershire, salt, and peppers and add to skillet; cover and simmer for 10 to 12 minutes longer.
6. Stir in cornstarch; cook and stir 2 to 3 minutes longer until sauce is thickened.
7. Serve over rice.
Serves five.
– Ken Keller
Lafayette, La.

# CRAB STEW

2 whole onions, diced
2 bell peppers, chopped
4 cloves garlic, chopped fine
1 stalk celery, chopped
1 tsp. Creole seasoning
1 cup roux
2 1/2 quarts water, divided

2 1/2 dozen cleaned crabs with
   claws, picked over for shells
   and cartilage
Green onion tops
Small bunch chopped parsley
Hot, cooked rice

1. Mix vegetables, seasoning, roux and one quart of the water in a large pot and cook over medium heat for 40 minutes, until vegetables are cooked.
2. Add crabmeat and claws and the remaining 1 1/2 quarts of water; season to taste.
3. Cook for 45 minutes over medium heat.
4. Just before serving, add onion tops and parsley. Serve over rice.
Serves six.
– Junior Lagneaux, Lagneaux's Restaurant
Lafayette

# FISH SAUCE PIQUANTE

2 medium onions, chopped
   fine
4 tbsp. cooking oil
1 (6-oz.) can tomato paste
1/2 tsp. sugar
1/2 cup chopped bell pepper
1/2 cup finely chopped celery

2 tbsp. finely chopped garlic
1 cup water
1/2 cup green onion tops
4 tbsp. chopped parsley
3 lbs. catfish or red fish, cut into
   chunks
Salt and pepper, to taste
Hot, cooked rice

1. In a large saucepan or Dutch oven over medium heat, sauté onions in oil until brown; add tomato paste and cook until oil separates and rises to top.
2. Add sugar and cook about 5 minutes.
3. Stir in bell pepper, celery and garlic and cook 5 minutes.
4. Add water and cook for 1 hour over low heat.
5. Stir in green onion tops, parsley, fish and salt and pepper to taste.
6. Cover pot and cook for a half hour.
7. Serve over rice.
– Darrell Patin
*Granny's Cajun Cookin'*

# TURTLE SAUCE PIQUANTE

4 onions, chopped
2 bell peppers, chopped
4 stalks celery, chopped
1 cup roux
1/2 cup ketchup
1 (14.5-oz.) can tomatoes
1 (15-oz.) can tomato sauce
1 head garlic, minced
Salt and pepper, to taste

4 quarts water
4 to 5 lbs. raw turtle meat
4 sour pickles, chopped
1 cup chopped stuffed olives
1 lemon, cut in wedges
2 oz. Worcestershire sauce
1 cup burgundy wine
Hot, cooked rice

1. Sauté onions, bell peppers and celery in a large soup pot in roux.
2. Add ketchup, tomatoes, tomato sauce, garlic, salt, pepper and water and bring to a boil.
3. Add turtle meat. Cook slowly until meat falls off the bones adding water if necessary, about 2 hours.
4. Add pickles, olives, lemon and Worcestershire sauce.
5. Cook until lemon is soft, about 20 minutes. Stir in wine.
6. Serve over rice.
– Mrs. Norma Clark Fruge
Crowley, La.

# FRIED CRAWFISH OR SHRIMP

Salt and pepper, to taste
1/2 tsp. garlic powder
1/2 tsp. onion salt
1 tsp. Creole seasoning

2 1/2 cups all-purpose flour
2 eggs
1/2 cup evaporated milk
2 lbs. peeled crawfish tails
Oil for deep-frying

1. Mix all seasoning with flour.
2. In a separate bowl, beat eggs with milk.
3. Dip crawfish tails in egg mixture, then in the flour.
4. Fry tails in hot oil until light brown, which takes only about 2 to 3 minutes. Be careful not to overcook!
Serves four.

# CAJUN CRAWFISH BOIL

Editor's Note: Having a crawfish boil is a major south Louisiana social event. Families get together for a back yard crawfish boil during crawfish season, which is from Thanksgiving to mid-June, with the peak of the season in April. The kids find it fun to play with the crawfish, to dare each other to pick one up without getting pinched. Cover the tables with newspaper or disposable, plastic tablecloths, get a platter full of crawfish, some ketchup with hot sauce in it for dipping, and start peeling. There's nothing else like it!

## EQUIPMENT:
- One very large pot, approximately 18 to 20 gallons, with cover.
- One propane burner big enough to easily bring this pot full of water to a boil.
- A large utensil used to stir the pot (a small paddle, broom handle, or thick, cleaned branch cut to about 3 feet).

## INGREDIENTS (IN ORDER OF USE):
1 (26-oz.) box salt (for cleaning crawfish)
1 (73-oz.) jar sack-size crab boil seasoning,
    or 10 (3-oz.) bags crab boil
1 oz. whole bay leaves, optional
5 to 10 lbs. small red potatoes (close to golf ball size or cut
    into quarters)
4 large lemons, cut into halves
5 large yellow onions, cut into quarters
24 oz. fresh mushrooms (small to medium-size whole ones),
    optional
1 (40-lb.) sack live Louisiana crawfish
12 half-pieces of corn-on-the-cob, preferably fresh

## PREPARATION:
1. Thoroughly wash crawfish in a large "foot tub" or ice chest by rinsing and draining twice, until rinse water is reasonably clean.
2. Cover crawfish in tub again with water, and add one-half pound of salt; the salt is added to purge and clean the crawfish prior to eating. Stir for no longer than 3 minutes and drain water.
3. Immediately fill the tub again with cool water, leaving out the salt, and stir for 3 minutes, then drain; if the crawfish are allowed to

soak in the water too long, they will die. Inspect and discard dead crawfish, bait and other debris that may be present.

## COOKING:

1. For a 40-lb. sack of crawfish, fill an 18- to 20-gallon pot with about 10 gallons of water, or enough water to cover crawfish and vegetables when they are put in. Bring to a boil.
2. Add crawfish boil seasoning. Bring mixture to a boil.
3. In the basket that fits into the pot, place bay leaves, potatoes, lemons, onions, mushrooms, and garlic.
4. Place the basket in the boiling water, and boil vegetables and seasonings for 15 to 20 minutes, or until tender, stirring occasionally.
5. Carefully add live crawfish to the basket, which is already in the pot of boiling water.
6. Stir, cover, and bring back to a boil. Once boiling, remove cover and let the whole thing boil for 4 minutes.
7. Remove entire pot from heat (with basket in it), or turn off heat; add corn. Stir and keep uncovered for 5 to 20 minutes. The longer the crawfish are left to stand like this (in excess of 5 minutes), the more seasoned and spicy they will be. You also want to cook them long enough to release them from their shell to make peeling them easier.
8. Start sampling (tasting) the crawfish after 5 minutes (of standing) to achieve the desired taste and consistency. Personally, we recommend that you let the crawfish stand covered until they begin to sink, which means they are thoroughly marinated with the water and seasonings, which is somewhere around 15 to 20 minutes. They should be quite spicy by that time, so be careful.

## MODIFICATIONS:

Divide ingredients and make 2 batches in order to perfect the second batch and keep crawfish nice and hot. Use less spices (or take some crawfish out earlier). Use more corn and potatoes for the less imaginative members of your group.

## COCKTAIL SAUCE:

Basically ketchup and horseradish, or ketchup with hot sauce, or lemon, butter, garlic, or any combination of the above.
Serves 10 to 20 people.
– Charley & Ruth Addison
*Cooking With Crazy Charley Part 3*

# CRABMEAT IMPERIAL

10 tbsp. butter, divided
2 tbsp. chopped bell pepper
2 tbsp. chopped pimento
9 tbsp. flour
1 1/2 tsp. salt
Red & black pepper, to taste
Paprika, to taste
3 cups milk
3 eggs yolks, beaten
1 1/2 tsp. dry mustard
1/8 tsp. paprika
1/2 cup capers, drained
1/8 tsp. black pepper
1 tbsp. Worcestershire sauce
6 tbsp. mayonnaise, divided
3 lbs. fresh lump crabmeat, well drained and picked over for shells and cartilage

1. Melt 1 tablespoon of butter in a small skillet. Sauté bell pepper and pimento for 3 to 5 minutes. Set aside.
2. In a large saucepan melt the remaining 9 tablespoons of butter.
3. Stir in flour, salt, peppers and paprika to taste. Stir until smooth.
4. Stir in milk slowly to make a sauce. Cook, stirring constantly until smooth and thick.
5. Stirring constantly, add a small amount of the sauce to egg yolks and mix well. Continue stirring in more sauce until about a cup of sauce has been added to egg yolks, mixing well after each addition. Add egg yolk mixture back to sauce in pan, stirring constantly.
6. Then stir in mustard, paprika, capers, pepper, Worcestershire sauce, 3 tablespoons of the mayonnaise, and the green pepper mixture. Blend well.
7. Fold in crabmeat.
8. Turn crabmeat mixture into a greased 2 1/2-quart casserole dish. Spread top with remaining 3 tablespoons of mayonnaise.
9. Bake uncovered at 350 degrees for about 30 minutes, or until golden on top.

Makes about 12 servings.
– Shirley Varisco Dieckman

# CRAWFISH & EGGPLANT CASSEROLE

2 eggplants, peeled and cubed
2 cups raw rice
Salt and red pepper, to taste
1 stick butter
1/4 cup chopped bell pepper
2 cloves garlic, minced
1 cup chopped onion
2 lbs. peeled crawfish tails
1/2 cup chopped green
onion tops
1/3 cup chopped parsley
1 (10.75-oz.) can condensed
cream of mushroom soup
1 (10.75-oz.) can condensed
cream of celery soup
1/2 cup breadcrumbs, toasted
Italian breadcrumbs

1. Cook eggplants in water, seasoned to taste, until tender. Drain and mash.
2. Cook rice according to package instructions and set aside.
3. In a saucepan, melt butter and sauté bell pepper, garlic and onion until soft.
4. Add crawfish tails, onion tops, and parsley. Cook over low heat 10 to 15 minutes or until vegetables are tender.
5. Add cooked and mashed eggplant, soups, rice, and breadcrumbs; stir well and season to taste.
6. Pour into a greased 3-quart casserole dish and sprinkle with Italian breadcrumbs.
7. Bake uncovered at 350 degrees for 30 minutes.
Note: Casserole may be refrigerated or frozen and baked later.
Serves six to eight.
– Annie Gautreaux, Ruby Hopkins, and Janet P. Stemmans

# TROUT SUPREME

10 speckled trout fillets, or any firm, white fish
Tony's Creole seasoning, to taste
1 bottle Italian dressing
2 onions, sliced and separated into rings
3 bell peppers, sliced into rings
1 jar sliced jalapeno peppers
1 stick butter, sliced into 1/8-inch pats
2 lemons, cut in half
1 (12- to 16-oz.) package shredded Monterey Jack cheese with jalapenos
1 (12- to 16-oz.) package shredded mozzarella cheese
10 slices American cheese

1. Season fillets with Creole seasoning, then marinate in Italian dressing for 24 hours.
2. Arrange fillets on a large baking dish and season again with Creole seasoning and top with onions, bell peppers, jalapenos and pats of butter.
3. Squeeze lemons over the fish, then cover with aluminum foil and bake for 20 minutes at 350 degrees; remove foil, and bake for 10 minutes longer.
4. Or, cook fillets on a hot grill with mesquite to give dish a smoked flavor.
5. Mix Monterey Jack and mozzarella cheese and sprinkle on top of fillets.
6. Top with slices of American cheese and return fillets to oven (or grill) until cheese has melted.

Serves 10.
– Adam Trahan
Silver Medal, *Le Petite Classique*

# FRIED FROG LEGS

2 lbs. frog legs
2 tsp. salt
1/4 tsp. pepper
2 eggs, beaten
4 tsp. lemon juice

2 tbsp. water
1/4 cup yellow corn meal
1 cup fine breadcrumbs
Cooking oil

1.  Season frog legs with salt and pepper.
2.  In a bowl, combine eggs, lemon juice and water.
3.  Dip frog legs into egg mixture, then roll in corn meal and breadcrumbs.
4.  Fry in oil (350 degrees) for 8 to 10 minutes or until golden brown and tender.

Makes four to five servings.
– Jackie Manuel


# OYSTER STEW

1 (10 1/2-oz.) can golden
    mushroom soup or 1/2 can
    condensed cream of
    mushroom soup
1 glass milk
12 raw oysters

Parsley
2 or 3 sprigs green onion tops,
    chopped
Salt and pepper, to taste
Crackers

1. Mix soup and milk and bring to a boil.
2. Add oysters, parsley, onion, salt and pepper and cook until soup thickens, adding more milk if needed.
3. Serve with crackers.
Makes two hearty servings.
– Junior Lagneaux, Lagneaux's Restaurant
Lafayette

# CRAWFISH SAUCE PICANTE

You can make this dish with crawfish, fish or shrimp.

1 medium onion, chopped
1/2 bell pepper, chopped
2 cloves garlic, minced
1/2 cup cooking oil
1 (10.75-oz.) can condensed
  cream of mushroom soup
1 (8-oz.) can tomato sauce

Water, as needed
Salt, to taste
Red and black pepper, to taste
1 lb. peeled crawfish tails
1/2 cup chopped onion tops
1/4 cup chopped parsley
Hot, cooked rice

1. Sauté onion, bell pepper and garlic in oil until soft.
2. Add soup, tomato sauce, water and seasonings and bring to a boil; reduce heat to medium and cook 10 minutes.
3. Add crawfish, onion tops and parsley and cook until crawfish is done.
4. Serve over rice.
– Lena Vasseur

# BAKED SHRIMP

1 lb. peeled, deveined shrimp
2 tbsp. butter
1 cup fresh breadcrumbs
2 tbsp. chopped parsley
1 small green onion, minced

1/4 cup minced garlic
1/2 tsp. dried thyme, crushed
1/2 tsp. dried tarragon, crushed
1/4 tsp. ground nutmeg
1/4 cup dry sherry

1. Cook shrimp and arrange in a buttered 10 x 6 x 2-inch baking dish.
2. Melt butter in an 8-inch skillet; turn off heat and stir in remaining ingredients. Sprinkle over shrimp.
3. Bake in a preheated 400-degree oven until hot, about 10 minutes.
Makes four servings.
– Dolores McFarlain

# STUFFED SHRIMP

## *SEAFOOD STUFFING*

1/4 cup butter
1/2 cup cooking oil
2 cups chopped onion
1/2 cup chopped bell pepper
1 cup chopped celery
1/4 cup chopped green onion
1 lb. chopped, uncooked shrimp

2 slices stale bread, toasted
Water
1 lb. crabmeat, picked over for
   shells and cartilage
2 eggs, beaten
Salt and pepper, to taste
Garlic powder, to taste

## *STUFFED SHRIMP*

4 lbs. large shrimp, peeled and deveined
Beaten egg mixed with milk
Flour
Oil for deep-frying

1. To make Stuffing, melt butter in saucepan; add oil. When oil is hot, add vegetables and sauté until wilted.
2. Add chopped shrimp and cook until done.
3. Soak bread in water; squeeze water out, mash bread, then add to shrimp mixture.
4. Add crabmeat and eggs and cook one full minute; mix well and season to taste.
5. Fantail large shrimp, not cutting through them.
6. Spoon Stuffing into shrimp; cover and freeze.
7. When ready to cook, dip shrimp in beaten egg with milk and roll in flour.
8. Fry in hot oil until done.
– Bootsie John Landry
*The Best of South Louisiana Cooking*

# SEAFOOD JAMBALAYA
# IN RICE COOKER

1 lb. peeled shrimp, crawfish, oysters or crab meat
1 (10.5-oz.) can chicken broth
1 1/4 cups (10 oz.) raw rice
1/2 stick butter

Salt and pepper, to taste
1 stalk celery, chopped
1 onion, finely chopped
1 bell pepper, finely chopped
1/2 cup chopped green onion
4 cloves garlic, minced

1. Stir together all ingredients in a rice cooker and turn on cooker.
2. After cooker shuts off, let stand 10 minutes before serving. Good with a salad.
NOTE: This meal will cook in 30 minutes and makes six one-cup servings.
– Terri Mouton Lancon

# CRAB ÉTOUFFÉE

3/4 stick real butter
1/3 cup chopped celery
1/2 cup chopped onion
1/2 cup chopped bell pepper (green or mixed)
1 tbsp. minced garlic
1 (10-oz.) can cream of mushroom with roasted garlic

1/2 (10- oz. can) cream of shrimp
1 1/2 - 2 cups water
1 tsp. Cajun seasoning, divided
10 to 16 oz. lump crabmeat, picked over for shells and cartilage
1/2 tsp. paprika (for color)
4 tbsp. finely chopped green onions

1. In a non-stick skillet, melt butter on medium heat and sauté vegetables until wilted, about 5 minutes.
2. Add cream of mushroom, cream of shrimp, water, and 1/2 teaspoon Cajun seasoning. Let simmer 10-15 minutes.
3. Carefully fold in crabmeat as to not break it apart.
4. Add additional seasoning and water to desired taste and thickness.
5. Add paprika and green onions and let simmer 2 to 3 more minutes.
Serve over hot rice and garnish with any remaining green onions.
–Cliff & Amy Amox
Arnaudville, La.

# SHRIMP & EGGPLANT CASSEROLE

3 medium eggplants, peeled and cubed
2 medium onions, chopped
1/2 medium bell pepper, chopped
1 tsp. minced garlic
1/2 stick butter

1 lb. small shrimp, peeled and deveined
1 cup cooked rice, optional
2 eggs, beaten
1/2 cup grated Parmesan cheese
Seasoning, to taste
1/2 cup breadcrumbs

1. Boil eggplants in water until tender. Drain and remove most of the seeds.
2. In a skillet, sauté onions, bell pepper, and garlic in butter.
3. Add shrimp, eggplant, rice, eggs and cheese; mix together well. Add seasonings to taste.
4. Place in a 2-quart casserole dish and top with breadcrumbs.
5. Bake uncovered at 350 degrees for 40 minutes, or until topping is brown.

Serves six to eight.
– Glenda Matt

# SHRIMP ÉTOUFFÉE

1 stick butter
1 cup chopped onion
2 small cloves garlic, minced
1/2 cup chopped bell pepper
1/2 cup of chopped celery
1 tbsp. tomato paste
1/2 tsp. cornstarch

1/2 cup warm water
2 lbs. shrimp, peeled and deveined
1/2 cup chopped green onion tops
1 cup chopped parsley
Salt and pepper, to taste
Hot, cooked rice

1. In a large saucepan over medium heat, melt butter and add onion, garlic, bell pepper, celery and tomato paste. Cook until vegetables are wilted.
2. Dissolve cornstarch in water. Add to mixture; cook and stir for 5 minutes.
3. Add shrimp and cook 20 to 25 minutes.
4. Add onion tops, parsley and seasonings and cook for 5 minutes more.
5. Serve over rice.
– Mrs. Edith Doucet

# CRAWFISH ÉTOUFFÉE

1 stalk celery, chopped
1 small bell pepper, chopped
1 onion, chopped
1 stick butter
3 tbsp. flour

1 lb. peeled crawfish tails with fat
1 (14-oz.) can chicken broth
Favorite seasonings, to taste
1 cup finely chopped green onion
Hot, cooked rice

1. Sauté celery, bell pepper, and onion in butter.
2. Add flour and stir constantly, but do not brown.
3. Add crawfish, broth, and favorite seasonings and mix well. Simmer for 25 minutes.
4. Stir in green onion and serve over rice.
5. Serves four.
– Danny Bonaventure

# CRAWFISH STEW

1 stick butter
3 tbsp. all-purpose flour
1 medium onion, chopped
1 medium bell pepper, chopped
2 stalks celery, chopped
2 cloves garlic, chopped fine

1 tbsp. Worcestershire sauce
1 lb. peeled crawfish tails with fat
Salt and pepper, to taste
Water, as needed
Hot, cooked rice
1 tbsp. chopped green onion tops

1. Make a roux with butter and flour in a non-reactive Dutch oven (do not use black iron pot). Cook until roux turns the color of chocolate.
2. Remove from heat and add all the vegetables and Worcestershire sauce. Stir mixture until it stops sizzling.
3. Add seasoned crawfish and enough water to cover all ingredients. Let simmer for 30 minutes or until done.
4. Serve over hot rice and garnish with onion tops.
Makes four generous servings.
Note: More crawfish can be added without altering ingredients. You can also substitute shrimp, crabmeat, oysters, clams or even fish fillets and get excellent results.
– Judy Dietz

# SHRIMP STEW

5 tbsp. butter
1 onion, chopped
1 small bell pepper, chopped
2 stalks celery, chopped fine
4 garlic cloves, chopped
1/2 (6-oz.) can tomato paste or
   sauce

1 cup roux
8 cups boiling water
Bootsie's Seasoning Salt
1 tsp. red pepper
2 lbs. peeled and deveined
   shrimp
Hot, cooked rice

1. In a skillet, melt butter and sauté onion, bell pepper, celery, and garlic for 20 minutes.
2. Add tomato paste and continue cooking on medium heat for 30 minutes.
3. In a large pot, add roux to boiling water and dissolve, then stir in sautéed vegetables and seasoning.
4. Cook for one hour, then add shrimp.
5. Bring sauce back to a boil, and cook for 15 minutes longer.
6. Serve over rice.

Serves eight.

Optional: Can also add cleaned boiled crabs to the above recipe for Crab and Shrimp Stew.

– Bootsie John Landry
*The Best of South Louisiana Cooking*

# STUFFED CRABS

**18 crabs, washed and cleaned**

## *SEASONED WATER*

Crab boil
Salt and pepper
Onion
Celery

Parsley
Hot pepper
Water to cover

## *STUFFING*

2 medium onions, minced
1/2 bell pepper, chopped
1 tbsp. butter
3 sprigs parsley, minced
2 green onions, minced
Crabmeat, picked over for
   shells and cartilage

1 tbsp. toasted breadcrumbs
3 tbsp. sweet cream
12 crab shells
Toasted breadcrumbs for topping
Lemon juice
Butter for topping

1. Boil crabs for one-half hour in Seasoned Water; pick crabmeat out of shells. Clean 12 of the shells and set aside.
2. To make Stuffing, sauté onions and bell pepper in butter until wilted; add parsley and green onions.
3. Add crabmeat and breadcrumbs and stir until thoroughly mixed. Cook for ten minutes.
4. Remove from heat and stir in cream.
5. Spoon Stuffing into crab shells. Top with toasted breadcrumbs.
6. Put about 10 drops of lemon juice and a small lump of butter on each crab. Bake in oven, uncovered, until tops are brown.

– Florence Gauthier

# DRESSINGS & BREADS

## RICE DRESSING (DIRTY RICE)

1 1/2 cups chopped green bell pepper
2 cups chopped onion
1 cup chopped celery
1 cup chopped mushrooms, optional
1/4 cup minced garlic
1 cup hog lard or cooking oil
2 tsp. brown sugar

3 lbs. ground round
1 lb. ground pork
1/2 lb. finely chopped chicken liver
3 tbsp. Cajun seasoning
6 1/2 cups water
2 tbsp. roux
1 tsp. Kitchen Bouquet
8 cups hot, cooked rice

1. In a 9-quart Dutch oven, mix bell pepper, onion, celery, mushrooms, garlic, and cooking oil. Sauté over medium-high heat for 15 minutes.
2. Add brown sugar and sauté for 4 to 5 minutes longer. Remove vegetables from pot but strain grease back into pot.
3. Add ground beef, pork, chicken liver, and Cajun seasoning and brown well.
4. Return vegetables to meat mixture. Add water, roux, and Kitchen Bouquet, mix well. Turn heat to high and bring to a boil, then lower heat to medium-high and cook at least 45 minutes. Taste occasionally and add additional seasoning as desired.
5. Slowly mix hot cooked rice into meat mixture to desired consistency.

–Cliff & Amy Amox
Arnaudville, La.

# CRAWFISH CORNBREAD

2 eggs
1 tsp. baking soda
1 small bell pepper, chopped
1/2 cup cooking oil
1/4 to 1/2 cup chopped
   jalapenos
1 large can creamed corn
   with pimentos

1 cup shredded Cheddar cheese
1 tsp. salt
1 medium onion, chopped
1 or 2 stalks celery, chopped
1 cup yellow corn meal
1 lb. peeled crawfish tails

1. Mix all together in large bowl and pour into greased casserole dish and bake for 30 minutes at 375 degrees.
2. Allow to cool for about 5 minutes before cutting into slices.
– Jeanne Saal

# COUCHE-COUCHE

Pronounced "koosh-koosh," this is an old-time traditional Cajun breakfast. It is the Cajun version of fried cornmeal mush.

Vegetable oil
2 cups yellow corn meal

1 cup water
Pinch of salt

1. In a black iron skillet, pour enough oil to coat bottom and sides. Turn heat to medium-high.
2. In a mixing bowl, stir together corn meal, salt, and just enough water so mixture is thicker than it is watery. Let stand about five minutes so corn meal can absorb water. Corn meal should be thick enough that a round ball can be made and barely hold together.
3. Once oil is hot, pour mixture into skillet; stir and scrape bottom and sides to prevent sticking and burning.
4. Cook for about 20 to 30 minutes or until golden brown.
5. Serve in a bowl with milk and butter; sweeten with syrup, sugar, or canned figs.
–Norbert Trahan
Kaplan, La.

# FRENCH BREAD

2 packages granular yeast
1/4 cup warm water
1 1/4 cups ice cold water

1 tbsp. sugar
2 tsp. salt
1 1/2 tbsp. shortening
5 cups sifted flour, divided

1. Dissolve yeast in warm water; set it aside.
2. Place ice water, sugar, salt and shortening in mixing bowl and blend well with electric mixer.
3. Add half the flour and beat until blended.
4. Add dissolved yeast and remaining flour until mixture forms a stiff dough and pulls away from side of bowl.
5. Let the dough rise in warm place until doubled.
6. Punch down; let rise 15 minutes then shape into long loaves with your hands.
7. Place on baking sheet and let rise until doubled.
8. With a sharp knife, cut a small slit down the length of each loaf to form a crease.
9. Brush the tops with cold water (or egg white beaten with a little water).
10. Bake at 375 degrees for 15 minutes until nicely browned.
Makes two to four loaves, depending on size of loaves.
– Mrs. Clyde Prather

# CORNBREAD DRESSING

1 chicken
1/2 stick butter
1 large onion, finely
chopped
1 bell pepper, chopped

3 stalks celery, chopped
3 bay leaves
Salt and pepper, to taste
2 eggs, beaten
1 (8 x 10-inch) pan of cornbread

1. Cut chicken into pieces and remove skin. Cover with water and
   bring to a boil.
2. Add butter, onion, bell pepper, celery, bay leaves, salt, and
   pepper. Boil until chicken falls apart. Cool chicken, de-bone, and
   dice small. Reserve chicken stock.
3. Break cornbread into large bowl. Gradually add enough chicken
   stock to cornbread to make mixture very moist. Adjust seasoning.
4. Stir eggs and enough chicken into mixture for desired consistency;
   spoon into casserole dish.
5. Bake, uncovered, at 350 degrees for one-half hour.
Serves 15 to 20.
– Gloria Boudreaux

# OLDE-FASHIONED BISCUITS

Editor's Note: Keller's Bakery has been a landmark in downtown
Lafayette since 1929, and the biscuits made from an old family recipe
are as popular as ever. This is the scaled-down version.

1 1/3 cups all-purpose flour
1 1/2 tsp. baking powder
1/2 tsp. salt

1 1/2 tbsp. granulated sugar
5 tbsp. butter
5 oz. cold milk

1. In a two-quart bowl, mix dry ingredients together well.
2. Using a pastry cutter or two knives, cut the butter or margarine
   into the dry ingredients. Be careful not to over mix. You want to
   see flakes of butter about the size of a dime.

3. Add milk and again be careful not to over mix. Mix just until all dry ingredients disappear. You should still be able to see small pieces of butter. Dough will be sticky.
4. On a lightly floured surface, roll dough out to a half-inch thickness.
5. Cut into 2 1/2-inch circles and place one inch apart on a baking sheet.
6. Bake in a pre-heated, 450-degree oven for eight to ten minutes, or until bottoms brown lightly.
7. Makes 10 biscuits.
– Ken Keller
Keller's Bakery
Lafayette, La.

# TASSO DRESSING

1/2 lb. ground tasso
1 lb. ground pork
Salt and pepper, to taste
1 cup chopped onion
1 cup chopped celery
1 cup chopped bell pepper
3 cloves garlic, minced
1 (10.5-oz.) can condensed
   mushroom soup

1 1/2 cups water
1 large can mushrooms, sliced
6 cups cooked rice
1 (1-lb.) container frozen dressing
   mix, thawed
3/4 cup chopped onion tops
1/4 cup chopped parsley

1. Season meat well and brown slightly in a large heavy Dutch oven.
2. Add vegetables and cook until vegetables are tender.
3. Add soup and water; cook on medium heat 20 to 25 minutes.
4. Add mushrooms, rice, dressing mix, onion tops, parsley and more seasoning if desired. Cook on low heat 10 minutes longer. If dressing should be too dry, add a little more water.
Note: This dressing is really good to stuff cabbage leaves or green peppers with.
– "Bit" Reed

# HOMEMADE BREAD

1 cup whole milk
1 cup water
1 tbsp. cooking oil
1 tbsp. butter
2 tbsp. sugar

1 tbsp. salt
1/4 cup lukewarm water
1 package active dry yeast
6 1/2 cups all-purpose flour

1. Warm the milk in a saucepan, then remove from heat. Add water, oil, butter, sugar, and salt; mix well.
2. Pour lukewarm water into a large bowl and stir in yeast until dissolved; add milk mixture.
3. Stir in three cups flour. Beat one minute, then work in remaining flour one cup at a time.
4. Shape dough into a ball and place in a greased bowl, turning once. Cover with a cloth and let rise in a warm place for one hour or until double in bulk.
5. Punch dough down, knead lightly, and divide into two loaves. Place in two greased loaf pans. Cover and let the dough rise again until doubled in bulk.
6. Bake for 10 minutes at 450 degrees. Reduce heat to 350 degrees and bake 30 minutes or until bread sounds hollow when lightly tapped. Remove bread from pans immediately and cool on wire racks.

Makes two loaves.

# OYSTER RICE DRESSING

2 large tbsp. roux
5 medium onions, chopped
1 bell pepper, chopped
1 hot pepper, chopped, optional
1 mild pepper, chopped, optional
2 stalks celery, chopped
1 lb. lean ground pork
3 lbs. ground beef

1 lb. chicken livers, chopped fine, optional
1 lb. chicken giblets, chopped fine, optional
3 cups raw rice, cooked
1 cup water
4 dozen oysters
1 quart chopped green onion tops

1. Melt roux in large, heavy pot.
2. Add onions, bell pepper, other peppers, and celery. Cook until vegetables are wilted.

3. Add pork and ground beef. Let cook on very low heat for two hours, stirring occasionally.
4. Add livers and giblets, if using, and cook 30 minutes longer.
5. Add cooked rice. Mix well.
6. Add water to keep mixture moist, but not runny.
7. When you are ready to serve, add oysters and green onion tops.
8. Let cook until oysters are done, about 5 to 10 minutes.
Serves 16.
 – Gina Calogero

# SWEET POTATO BREAD

2/3 cup shortening
2 2/3 cups sugar
4 eggs
1 (16-oz.) can sweet potatoes, drained and mashed
2/3 cup water
3 1/3 cups flour

2 tsp. baking soda
1 1/2 tsp. salt
1/2 tsp. baking powder
1 tsp. ground cinnamon
1 tsp. ground cloves
2/3 cup coarsely chopped nuts
2/3 cup raisins

1. Preheat oven to 350 degrees.
2. In a large bowl, cream shortening and sugar until fluffy.
3. Stir in eggs, sweet potato and water.
4. Combine flour, soda, salt, baking powder, cinnamon, and cloves; stir into sweet potato mixture.
5. Stir in nuts and raisins.
6. Pour into two greased 9 x 5 x 3-inch loaf pans.
7. Bake about 70 minutes, until wooden pick inserted in center comes out clean.
 – Mrs. George Sobiesk

# CRAWFISH CORNBREAD DRESSING

1 stick butter
1 large white onion, chopped
1 large bell pepper, chopped
2 lbs. peeled crawfish tails
1 tsp. hot sauce
1/2 cup water

Salt and pepper, to taste
1/4 cup chopped parsley
1/4 cup chopped green onions
1 tsp. cornstarch dissolved in 1/4
    cup water, to thicken
Cornbread (Recipe follows)

1. Melt butter in a black iron skillet.
2. Sauté onion and bell pepper until limp.
3. Add crawfish, hot sauce, water, salt and pepper, and cook on low for 15 minutes.
4. Add parsley, onion tops, and cornstarch mixture.
5. Cook on low for 10 minutes, stirring occasionally.
6. Break cornbread into small pieces, and fold into crawfish mixture.
7. Spoon dressing into a greased 2 1/2-quart baking dish; bake at 350 degrees for about 30 to 40 minutes or until hot.
Serves eight.

## CORNBREAD

1 cup yellow cornmeal
1 cup all-purpose flour
1/4 cup sugar
4 tsp. baking powder
1/2 tsp. salt

1 cup milk
1 egg
1/4 cup vegetable shortening,
    melted

1. Combine corn meal, flour, sugar, baking powder, and salt.
2. Add milk, egg and shortening; beat until fairly smooth.
3. Pour into a greased 8-inch iron skillet, and bake in a preheated 425-degree oven, for 20 to 25 minutes.
– Julie M. McCarthy

# PUMPKIN BREAD

3 cups sugar
1 cup oil
4 eggs
2 cups mashed pumpkin
1 (6-oz.) can orange juice
    concentrate, thawed
3 1/2 cups sifted flour
2 tsp. baking soda

1 tsp. baking powder
1 1/2 tsp. salt
2 tsp. cinnamon
2 tsp. nutmeg
1/2 tsp. cloves
1 tsp. allspice
1 cup nuts

1. Cream sugar and oil.
2. Add eggs and beat well.
3. Add pumpkin and orange juice; beat well.
4. Combine dry ingredients and stir into pumpkin mixture.
5. Pour into two greased loaf pans. Bake at 350 degrees for one hour.
Note: Can use boiled sweet potato instead of pumpkin.
– Laura Crouch

# PERSIMMON BREAD

2 eggs
3/4 cup sugar
1/2 cup vegetable oil
1 tsp. baking soda
1 cup persimmon pulp

1 1/2 cups all-purpose flour
1 tsp. ground cinnamon
1/2 tsp. salt
1/2 cup chopped pecans or
    walnuts
1/2 cup raisins, optional

1. Preheat oven to 325 degrees.
2. In a large bowl, mix eggs, sugar and oil.
3. In a small bowl, mix soda with persimmon pulp. Add to sugar
   mixture.
4. Combine flour, cinnamon, salt, chopped nuts and raisins and fold
   into persimmon mixture.
5. Pour batter into oiled or sprayed 9 x 4 x 3-inch loaf pan.
6. Bake at 325 degrees for one hour and fifteen minutes.
– Mary Floyd
Kaplan, La.

# RICE & EGGPLANT DRESSING

1 lb. ground beef
1/2 lb. chicken livers and
    gizzards, chopped fine
1 large eggplant, peeled and
    diced

1/4 cup chopped bell pepper
1/2 cup chopped celery
1/2 cup chopped onion
3 cloves garlic, minced
Salt and pepper, to taste
2 cups cooked rice

1. In a large saucepan, cook ground beef, livers and gizzards.
2. Stir in eggplant, bell pepper, celery, onion, garlic, salt and pepper.
3. Simmer mixture until eggplant is cooked, about 25 minutes.
4. Stir in rice and serve. (More rice can be added if desired.)
– Johnnie Bobbett


# PAIN PERDU
## (LOST BREAD OR FRENCH TOAST)

2 eggs
1/2 cup milk
1 tsp. sugar
1/8 tsp. salt
4 slices stale bread

Butter
Cinnamon sugar
Syrup, optional
Powdered sugar, optional

1. Beat eggs until light and fluffy.
2. Add milk, sugar and salt and beat until well blended; pour into
   wide shallow bowl.
3. Melt some butter in a large skillet over medium heat.
4. Dip each side of bread into egg mixture and fry in butter until
   brown and puffy on both sides.
5. Top with melted butter and cinnamon sugar or syrup and or
   powdered sugar.
– Ruth Pousson
Egan, La.

# VEGETABLES & SIDE DISHES

## BAKED BEANS

1 (15.25-oz.) can baby lima beans
1 (16-oz.) can butter beans
1 (16-oz.) can red kidney beans
1 (15-oz.) can pork and beans

1 lb. bacon, cut into 1-inch pieces
1 medium onion, diced
1 cup packed brown sugar
1 cup water

1. Drain all beans except pork and beans and mix together.
2. Mix bacon and onion with brown sugar and water in a large saucepan. Bring to a boil and cook 10 minutes.
3. Add beans to bacon mixture and mix well. Pour into a 13 x 9-inch baking dish and bake, uncovered, at 350 degrees for 1 to 1 1/4 hours.

Serves six.
– Dolores Dallas

## BAKED POTATO CASSEROLE

5 to 6 large red or white potatoes
2 cups grated cheese
1 stick butter
Bacon bits or crispy real bacon

4 green onions, chopped, or chives in amount desired
Salt and pepper, to taste
Sour cream, as needed
Milk, if needed

1. Peel and boil potatoes. Drain.
2. Mash potatoes in a large bowl; stir in cheese, butter, bacon bits, onions or chives, and salt and pepper.
3. Add enough sour cream for desired flavor and consistency.
4. Stir in milk if needed for desired consistency.
5. Spoon potato mixture into a large casserole dish.
6. Bake at 350 degrees for 35 to 45 minutes. Can be topped with more cheese before baking.

– Marilyn Long

# CORN CASSEROLE

1 stick butter
1/2 cup chopped bell pepper
1/2 cup chopped onion
2 (14.75-oz.) cans whole kernel
corn, drained
1 (14.75-oz.) can cream-style
corn

1 egg, beaten
1 (10.75-oz.) can condensed
cream of mushroom soup
1/2 package saltine crackers,
finely crushed
3 slices cheddar cheese
1 (2.8-oz.) can onion rings,
crushed

1. Melt butter in a 2-quart casserole; add all remaining ingredients except onion rings and mix well.
2. Top with onion rings.
3. Bake at 350 degrees for 30 minutes.
Serves eight.
- Dolores Dallas

# CRAWFISH MAQUE CHOUX

1 onion, chopped
1 bell pepper, chopped
1 stalk celery, chopped
1 clove garlic, minced
1 stick butter
1 (15.25-oz.) can whole kernel
corn

1 (14.75-oz.) can cream-style corn
1 (10-oz.) can tomatoes with
green chilies
Seasonings, to taste
1 lb. peeled, deveined crawfish
tails
Hot, cooked rice

1. In a saucepan, sauté onion, bell pepper, celery and garlic in butter.
2. Add corn, tomatoes and seasonings and bring to a boil.
3. Add crawfish tails and simmer for 30 minutes.
Serve over rice.
Note: Shrimp or crabmeat can be substituted for crawfish.
- Audrey Lyons

# CANDIED YAMS

Editor's Note: This is my mom and dad's recipe, contributed by my sister Karen. Mom and Dad made these every year for our Thanksgiving get-togethers. I like to refrigerate them over night and serve them at room temperature the next day.

5 lbs. sweet potatoes
1 stick butter
1 (16-oz.) bottle light corn
   syrup
1 (5-oz.) can evaporated milk
Juice of 1 lemon

1 tsp. ground cinnamon, or
   to taste
1 to 1 1/2 cups coarsely broken
   pecans, toasted
1 (10-oz.) bag large
   marshmallows

1. Peel yams and cut into 2-inch chunks. Place in a large saucepan and cover with water. Bring to a boil; cover, reduce heat, and cook just until tender, about 30 minutes. Drain.
2. Meanwhile, melt butter in a large saucepan over low heat. Add corn syrup, evaporated milk, lemon juice, and cinnamon; mix well and set aside.
3. Arrange potatoes in a 13 x 9-inch baking pan and pour syrup over top. Bake in a 375-degree oven for 2 to 3 hours.
4. Sprinkle pecans over potatoes and top with marshmallows. Bake 5 to 10 minutes longer or until lightly browned.

Serves 12 to 15.
– Mrs. Edmay Stelly Bertrand
Opelousas, La.
Submitted by Karen B. Pilgreen

# CORN & GREEN BEAN CASSEROLE

1 (11-oz.) can shoe peg corn, drained
1 (14.5-oz.) can French-style green beans, drained
1/2 cup chopped celery
1/2 cup chopped bell pepper
1/2 cup chopped onion
1/2 cup sour cream
1 cup grated cheddar cheese
1 (10.75-oz.) can condensed cream of celery soup
Cracker Topping (Recipe follows)

1. Combine all ingredients except Topping and mix well.
2. Pour mixture into a greased, 2-quart casserole dish.
3. Prepare cracker topping and sprinkle over casserole; bake at 375 degrees for 1 hour.

## CRACKER TOPPING

1/2 stick butter
1-inch-square cheese crackers or crumbled Ritz crackers, enough to cover top of casserole

1. Melt butter and stir in cheese crackers or Ritz crackers.
– Ellen Carroll

# RICE

This is the old-fashioned method of cooking rice. Now, just about all Cajuns have a rice cooker, which practically prevents burned rice at the bottom of the pot.

2 cups uncooked rice
3 cups water
2 tbsp. oil or butter
1/2 tsp. salt

1. Rinse rice thoroughly in a deep pot and add the water, oil and salt.
2. Boil, uncovered, over medium-high heat until water level is even with rice.
3. Cover, turn heat to its lowest point, and cook 35 to 45 minutes.
– Junior Lagneaux, Lagneaux's Restaurant
Lafayette

# BROCCOLI CASSEROLE

1 stick butter
1 medium or large onion,
   finely chopped
1 roll of garlic-flavored cheese
1 (4.5-oz.) jar mushrooms,
   drained

1 (10.75-oz.) can cream of
   mushroom soup
Salt and pepper, to taste
1 large or 2 small bunches fresh
   broccoli, chopped and cooked
Seasoned breadcrumbs
Butter

1. Melt butter in a pan; add onion and sauté until transparent.
2. Add garlic cheese and stir until melted.
3. Add mushrooms, soup and seasonings and mix well.
4. Stir in broccoli.
5. Pour into greased au gratin dish and sprinkle seasoned
   breadcrumbs on top (not too much). Dot with butter.
6. Bake uncovered at 350 degrees for 20 to 35 minutes until bubbly.
Variations: add artichoke hearts or chopped, cooked cauliflower.
Serves four to six.
– Jill Spikes

# SWEET POTATO CASSEROLE

1 egg
1 cup sugar
1 stick butter, melted
1/2 cup milk

1/2 tsp. salt
2 cups fresh, grated sweet
potatoes
1/2 cup ground pecans

1. Beat egg, sugar, and butter together.
2. Add milk, salt, and sweet potato.
3. Pour into a 6 x 6-inch baking dish and bake uncovered at 325
   degrees for 30 minutes; sprinkle pecans and bake 30 minutes
   longer.
Serves eight.
– Maria Bienvenue

# SMOTHERED OKRA & TOMATOES

2 lbs. okra, sliced
3 tbsp. oil, divided
1 tbsp. flour
1 medium onion, chopped
1/2 green bell pepper, chopped

2 medium stalks celery, chopped
5 fresh tomatoes, chopped, or 1
  (28-oz.) can diced tomatoes
Tony's Creole Seasoning, or salt
  and pepper.

1. In a large, non-reactive skillet, fry okra in two tablespoons of oil until it is not sticky. *Do not* use a black iron pot.
2. In another skillet make a medium-dark roux with one tablespoon of oil and the flour.
3. Add onion, bell pepper and celery and simmer until wilted.
4. Add tomatoes and simmer for 5 minutes longer.
5. Add okra and season well.
6. Cook for one hour on low heat.

Serves six.

NOTE: Can be frozen for later use. Ideal for gumbos.

– Tony Chachere
*Tony Chachere's Cajun Country Cookbook*

# SQUASH CASSEROLE

1 lb. yellow squash
1 tsp. sugar
Water
5 tbsp. butter
1/2 cup chopped onion
1 cup chopped bell pepper

1/2 cup mayonnaise
1/2 cup grated cheddar cheese
1 egg, slightly beaten
1/2 cup chopped pimentos
10 unsalted crackers

1. Peel and cut squash into chunks, then boil in sugar and water, until tender; drain and mash with fork.
2. Preheat oven to 350 degrees.
3. In skillet, melt butter, and then remove one tablespoon of the butter, and set aside.

4. Add onion and bell pepper to remaining butter in skillet; cook until tender.
5. Add squash to skillet mixture, then fold in mayonnaise, cheese, egg and pimentos.
6. Spoon the mixture into a one-quart casserole dish.
7. Crush and mix crackers with remaining one tablespoon of butter and sprinkle over casserole.
8. Bake for thirty minutes or until brown.

# STUFFED BELL PEPPER

1/2 cup butter
1 medium onion, chopped
1 stalk celery, chopped
2 tbsp. chopped bell pepper
1/2 tsp. parsley flakes
1 1/2 lbs. ground chuck or 1 1/2 lbs. cleaned crawfish tails, whole

3 cloves garlic, minced
2 cups breadcrumbs, divided
2 tsp. Worcestershire sauce
2 eggs
1/2 cup evaporated milk
2 tsp. sugar
Salt and pepper, to taste
6 bell peppers, cleaned and parboiled, for stuffing

1. Melt butter in a large skillet, then sauté onion, celery, bell pepper and parsley. Cook several minutes.
2. Blend in meat and garlic. Cover and cook until meat is done, about 20 minutes. Add water if needed.
3. Stir in 1 1/2 cups of breadcrumbs and Worcestershire sauce.
4. Beat eggs and evaporated milk together in a bowl. Add to meat mixture, then add sugar, salt and pepper. If mixture is too dry, add more milk.
5. Spoon mixture into bell pepper shells. Sprinkle remaining half cup of breadcrumbs over tops. Bake at 400 degrees about 30 minutes or until brown.
Makes six servings.
– Johnnie Bobbett

# CORN MAQUE CHOUX

1/4 cup chopped onion
1/4 cup chopped celery
1/4 cup cooking oil
2 cups tomatoes with green
   chilies
1/4 cup chopped pimento

1 cup fresh or canned yellow corn
   kernels
1 cup fresh or canned white corn
   kernels
Garlic powder
Salt
Pinch of sugar

1. Sauté onion and celery in oil until wilted.
2. Add tomatoes and pimento and cook 20 minutes.
3. Add corn and season well.
4. Continue cooking until corn becomes tender.
Serves six.
Note: Use fresh corn when possible.
– Bootsie John Landry
*The Best of South Louisiana Cooking*

# FRIED EGGPLANT

4 medium eggs
3 small eggplants, peeled
Flour

Salt and cayenne pepper, to taste
Garlic and onion powder, to taste
3 tbsp. cooking oil
Mozzarella cheese

1. In a mixing bowl, beat eggs.
2. Slice eggplants 1/4-inch thick and soak in water; drain and dry.
3. Mix together flour and seasonings.
4. Dip eggplant slices into egg, then roll in flour mixture.
5. Heat oil in a skillet over medium heat. Add eggplant and cook
   until golden brown on both sides, about 10 minutes. Remove
   from pan and sprinkle with cheese.
Serve immediately.

# GREEN BEAN CASSEROLE

1 (10.75-oz.) can condensed cream of mushroom soup
1/2 cup milk
Pepper, to taste

2 (14.5-oz.) cans cut green beans, drained
1 (2.8-oz.) can French fried onion rings, divided

1. In a 1 1/2-quart casserole dish, mix soup, milk, pepper, beans and half of the onion rings.
2. Bake at 350 degrees for 30 minutes; remove from oven and stir.
3. Sprinkle the remaining onion rings on the top of the bean mixture.
4. Bake an additional 5 minutes or until onions are golden brown.
Serves six.

# SMOTHERED CABBAGE

1 package turkey tasso or smoked sausage
3 tbsp. cooking oil

1 medium head cabbage
1/4 cup cooking oil
1 tbsp. Cajun seasoning

1. In an 8-qt. non-reactive pot, sauté tasso in oil for 10-15 minutes until well browned.
2. Slice cabbage and add to pot.
3. Pour 1/4 cup cooking oil over cabbage and season. Stir, cover, and cook over medium heat 30 minutes, stirring occasionally.
Season to taste.
– Cliff & Amy Amox
Arnaudville, La.

# COUNTRY FRIED POTATOES

1/4 cup cooking oil
4 to 5 potatoes, sliced
1 large onion, sliced into rings
Salt and pepper, or Tony's
   Creole seasoning to taste

Cheddar Cheese
Sour cream
Chopped green onions
Bacon, cooked and crumbled

1. Heat the cooking oil in heavy skillet over low heat.
2. Arrange half of potatoes and onion in layers in skillet; sprinkle with seasoning and cheese.
3. Repeat layers with remaining potatoes, onion and seasoning; cover and cook for fifteen minutes. Do not stir.
4. Uncover and increase heat slightly; cook for ten minutes longer, or until potatoes are crisp and brown on the underside.
5. Fold in half, like an omelet, top with sour cream, green onions, and bacon pieces.

Serve on platter.

# STEWED OKRA

1/2 lb. bacon, diced
3 to 4 cups chopped okra
1 cup chopped onion
1/2 cup chopped parsley

1/2 cup chopped bell pepper
1 tsp. finely chopped garlic
Salt and pepper, to taste

1. Fry bacon and drain grease.
2. Add remaining ingredients and simmer until onions are tender, stirring often.

# STUFFED BAKED EGGPLANT OR MIRLITONS

3 medium-size eggplants or
   3 large mirlitons
1/2 cup chopped onion
1/4 cup chopped bell pepper
1/4 cup chopped celery
1/2 cup butter
1 cup chopped, cooked shrimp

1 cup white crabmeat
1 tbsp. chopped pimento
Salt, pepper and garlic powder, to
   taste
1/2 cup breadcrumbs
1/4 cup chopped green onion

1. Cut eggplants or mirlitons in half and steam until tender; cool, scoop out pulp and keep shells intact.
2. Brown vegetables in melted butter.
3. Add shrimp, crabmeat, pimento, seasoning and eggplant pulp. Mix well and cook 10 minutes.
4. Stir in breadcrumbs and green onion. Add more melted butter if mixture is too dry.
5. Spoon stuffing into eggplant shells. Sprinkle tops with additional breadcrumbs.
6. Bake uncovered at 350 degrees until hot.

– Bootsie John Landry
Cookbook Hall of Fame Winning Recipe
*The Best of South Louisiana Cooking*

## BEIGNETS
### *(CREOLE DOUGHNUTS)*

1/2 cup boiling water
2 tbsp. vegetable shortening
1/4 cup sugar
1/2 tsp. salt
1/2 cup evaporated milk
1 package dry yeast

1/4 cup warm water
1 egg, beaten
3 3/4 cups all-purpose flour, divided
Powdered sugar
Oil for deep-frying

1. Pour boiling water over shortening, sugar and salt in a small bowl; add milk and let stand until warm.
2. Dissolve yeast in warm water and add to milk mixture with the beaten egg.
3. Stir in two cups of the flour and beat well. Add enough additional flour to make a soft dough.
4. Place in a greased bowl and grease top of dough; cover with waxed paper and a cloth. Chill until ready to use.
5. Heat oil to 360 degrees. On a lightly floured surface, roll dough to 1/8-inch thickness. Do not let dough rise before frying.
6. Cut into squares and fry a few at a time in hot oil until brown on both sides.
7. Drain on absorbent paper and sprinkle with powdered sugar.
Makes about 30 beignets.
– Mrs. Cursey Vidrine

# BLACKBERRY COBBLER

2 quarts fresh or frozen blackberries
2 cups sugar, divided
1 stick butter, softened
2 eggs
1 tsp. vanilla
3 cups all-purpose flour

2 tsp. baking powder
1/2 tsp. salt
1/2 tsp. ground nutmeg
1 1/4 cups milk
Whipped cream, optional

1. Combine blackberries and 1 cup of the sugar in a large bowl and mix well.
2. In a large mixing bowl, cream together butter and remaining 1 cup of sugar. Beat in eggs, one at a time, and vanilla.
3. In another large bowl, combine flour, baking powder, salt, and nutmeg and blend well. Add to butter mixture alternately with milk, scraping down sides and beating until smooth.
4. Pour half of batter into a greased 13 x 9-inch baking pan. Spoon berry mixture evenly over batter and drizzle remaining batter evenly over berries.
5. Bake in a 375-degree oven for 45 minutes or until golden brown on top. Serve warm or at room temperature with whipped cream.

Serves 12 to 15.
– Curtis Bertrand
Opelousas, La.
Contributed by Karen B. Pilgreen

# BREAD PUDDING MUFFINS

1 (12-oz.) can evaporated milk
3 eggs
1 stick butter, melted
2 cups sugar
1 tbsp. vanilla

10 to 12 pieces stale bread, torn apart
1/2 cup raisins, optional
1 (15-oz.) can sweetened condensed milk, for sauce

1. Spray a 12-cup muffin pan with vegetable cooking spray until well coated.
2. Combine all ingredients, except condensed milk in a bowl and mix well.
3. Pour mixture into muffin pan, filling cups two-thirds full.
4. Bake at 350 degrees for 40 minutes or until done.
5. Take out of pan immediately to avoid sticking.
6. Serve with condensed milk spooned over top for sauce.
Makes 12.

# BREAD PUDDING

8 slices bread
4 cups warm milk, divided
1 (5-oz.) can evaporated milk

1 tsp. vanilla
2 cups plus 1 tbsp. sugar, divided
4 eggs, separated
1/2 stick butter, melted

1. In a bowl, soak bread in 1 cup of warm milk; squeeze out excess milk back into cup.
2. Pour remaining warm milk over bread.
3. Stir in evaporated milk, vanilla and 1 1/2 cups of the sugar.
4. In a separate bowl, beat 1 egg white; gradually beat in the 4 egg yolks.
5. Pour egg mixture and melted butter into bread mixture and mix well.
6. Pour into a greased pan and bake at 325 degrees for 40 minutes.
7. Beat the remaining 3 egg whites till stiff; add the remaining one-half cup plus 1 tablespoon of sugar gradually and beat well to make a meringue.
8. Spread over baked pudding and return to oven till brown.
– Velda Martin
Gueydan, La.

# YAM PIE DE LOUISIANNE

## *PIE DOUGH*

1 cup flour

1/8 tsp. salt

1/3 cup shortening

2 1/2 tbsp. water

1. Sift together flour and salt; cut in shortening until uniform.
2. Gradually stir in water with a fork and mix just until dough holds together.
3. Roll out on a lightly floured board with rolling pin until very thin. Makes pastry for a nine-inch pie.

## *FILLING*

1 1/4 cups mashed, cooked yams

1 cup sugar

1 tbsp. butter

3 eggs

1/2 cup evaporated milk

1. Combine yams, sugar and butter and beat well.
2. Add eggs one at a time, beating after each addition.
3. Stir in milk; pour into uncooked pastry shell.

## *TOPPING*

1/3 cup flour

1/3 cup butter, softened

1/2 cup dark brown sugar

1/3 cup oatmeal

1/4 cup finely chopped pecans

1/4 cup whole pecans

1. Mix all ingredients with fork until mixture is moist and holds together.
2. Topping is thick and will not spread over soft filling, so spread in a 7 to 8-inch circle shape on wax paper, then flip over onto pie filling. Sprinkle whole pecans on top.
3. Bake pie for 40 minutes at 350 degrees.

– Pat Gotte

# CAJUN SHEET CAKE

2 cups sugar
2 cups all-purpose flour
4 tbsp. cocoa
1 stick butter
1/2 cup shortening
1 cup water

1/2 cup buttermilk
2 eggs, slightly beaten
1 tsp. baking soda
1 tsp. vanilla
Icing (Recipe follows)

1. Mix sugar, flour and cocoa in a large mixing bowl.
2. Combine butter, shortening and water in a small saucepan and bring to a boil; add to dry ingredients and mix well.
3. Stir in buttermilk, eggs, soda and vanilla; mix well.
4. Pour batter into a greased 15 x 11 x 1-inch cake pan. Bake at 350 degrees for 20 to 25 minutes.
5. Five minutes before cake is done, prepare Icing.

## *ICING*

1 stick butter
3 oz. milk
4 tbsp. cocoa

1 (1 lb.) box powdered sugar
1 tsp. vanilla
1 cup finely chopped pecans, divided

1. Combine butter, milk and cocoa in a saucepan and bring to a boil.
2. Add powdered sugar and vanilla; mix well.
3. Stir in 1/2 cup of pecans and pour over hot cake.
4. Drizzle remaining pecans over top of cake.
– Iris Gotte

# CREAMY RICE PUDDING

1 1/2 quarts 2% milk
1 cup sugar
1/2 cup Mahatma or Water Maid rice

1/2 cup raisins
1 tsp. vanilla extract

1. Combine milk, sugar and rice in a heavy saucepan.
2. Bring to a gentle boil over medium heat.
3. Reduce heat to simmer and cook uncovered for one hour, stirring occasionally. (The milk should just barely simmer, with bubbles

breaking only at the outside edge of the surface. After an hour, the rice should be soft.)

4. Add raisins, and increase heat to medium.
5. Cook, stirring frequently, until rice has absorbed most of the rest of the milk, but not all, and the pudding is creamy (about 30 minutes longer).
6. Remove from heat and stir in vanilla extract.
7. When cool, pudding will thicken, but will still be very creamy.
8. Serve warm or well chilled.

Serves eight.

– Contributed by Riviana Foods

# CAJUN CAKE

2 cups flour
1 1/2 cups sugar
2 tsp. baking soda

1 (20-oz.) can crushed pineapple, drained
2 eggs, well beaten
Icing (Recipe follows)

1. Sift together the flour, sugar and soda into a bowl.
2. Add pineapple and eggs. Mix well using a spoon. Batter will be thick.
3. Pour into a greased 13 x 9-inch baking pan and bake at 350 degrees for 30 minutes or until done.
4. Meanwhile, prepare icing.

## *ICING*

1 stick butter
3/4 cup sugar
1/2 cup evaporated milk

1 cup shredded coconut
1 cup chopped pecans
1 tsp. vanilla

1. Melt butter in a small saucepan over low heat; stir in sugar and milk and bring to a boil.
2. Cook one minute, then add coconut, pecans and vanilla.
3. Punch holes in cake with a fork while cake is still hot. Spread icing over top.

– Jean Schexnider

# PECAN TASSIES

1/2 cup butter
3 oz. cream cheese

1 cup all-purpose flour
Pecan Filling (Recipe follows)

1. Preheat oven to 325 degrees.
2. To make the pastry, beat butter and cream cheese in a bowl until combined; stir in flour.
3. Place a rounded teaspoon of pastry evenly into bottom of ungreased 1 3/4-inch muffin cups and press evenly up sides.
4. Prepare Pecan Filling and spoon 1 heaping teaspoon into each pastry-lined cup.
5. Bake at 325 degrees for 30 minutes. Transfer to rack and cool completely.

## PECAN FILLING

1 egg
3/4 cup packed brown sugar

1 tbsp. melted butter
1/2 cup coarsely chopped pecans

1. In a mixing bowl beat egg, brown sugar and melted butter until combined, then stir in pecans.
– Erika Stevens

# OLD TIME BUTTERMILK PIE

1/2 cup butter, softened
2 cups sugar
3 rounded tbsp. flour
3 eggs, beaten

1 cup buttermilk
1 tsp. vanilla
Dash nutmeg, optional
9-inch unbaked pie shell

1. In a mixing bowl, combine butter and sugar and blend together well.
2. Add flour and eggs, and beat well.
3. Stir in buttermilk, vanilla and nutmeg.
4. Pour into unbaked pie shell and bake for 45 to 50 minutes at 350 degrees. Place on wire rack to cool.

# PEAR CAKE

1 1/2 sticks butter, softened
2 cups sugar
2 cups cooked, mashed pears
1 tsp. vanilla

3 cups all-purpose flour
1 tsp. cinnamon
1 1/2 tsp. baking soda

1. Cream butter and sugar together.
2. Add pears and vanilla and mix well.
3. Sift together flour, cinnamon and soda a little at a time and add to pear mixture. Dough will be stiff.
4. Pour into a greased and floured 10-inch Bundt pan.
5. Bake in 325-degree oven for 1 hour or until cake shrinks from side of pan.
6. Cool 10 minutes and turn onto wire rack.
– Mrs. Edith Doucet

# PUMPKIN PIE

1 (15-oz.) can pumpkin
1 tsp. ginger
1 tsp. nutmeg
1 tsp. salt
1 tsp. cinnamon

1 (15-oz.) can sweetened condensed milk
2 eggs
1/8 cup brown sugar
1 unbaked 9-inch deep-dish pie shell
Whipped cream

1. Combine all ingredients except pie shell and whipped cream; mix well and pour into pie shell.
2. Place pie on a cookie sheet and bake at 375 degrees for 40 minutes, or until knife inserted into center comes out clean.
3. Cool and garnish with whipped cream.
– Linden Bercegeay

# OLD-FASHIONED FIG CAKE

1/2 cup shortening
3 eggs
1 1/2 cups sugar
2 cups flour, sifted
1 tsp. baking soda
1 tsp. cinnamon
1 tsp. baking powder

1 tsp. cloves, optional
1/2 tsp. nutmeg
1 tsp. allspice, optional
1 cup buttermilk
1 cup chopped pecans, optional
2 cups fig preserves, chopped

1. Cream shortening, eggs and sugar together.
2. Add the flour, baking soda, cinnamon, baking powder, cloves, nutmeg and allspice, and mix well.
3. Stir in buttermilk, pecans and figs and mix together.
4. Pour mixture into a greased Bundt (tube) pan. Bake 30 minutes at 350 degrees or until done. No icing is needed.
   – Jean C. Schexnider

# PECAN PIE

1/2 cup melted butter
1 cup sugar
1 cup corn syrup
1/2 tsp. salt

1 1/2 tsp. vanilla
2 cups coarsely chopped pecans
3 eggs, beaten
1 unbaked (9-inch) pie shell

1. Melt butter in saucepan over low heat; add sugar, corn syrup and salt and stir until sugar dissolves.
2. Remove from heat and add vanilla and pecans.
3. Let cool, then stir in eggs.
4. Pour into the pie shell and bake about 50 minutes at 350 degrees.
   – Mildred Sturlese

# LES OREILLES DE COCHON
## (PIG'S EARS)

1 1/2 cups flour
1/4 tsp. salt
3/4 cup water

Oil for deep-frying
1 (12-oz.) can cane syrup

1. Mix flour and salt together; add water to make stiff dough.
2. Cut off a walnut-size portion and roll very thin on floured board; continue doing so until you use all the dough.
3. Fry pastry in hot oil, giving a swift twist to the center of each with a long-handled fork. (This forms the "ear.") Fry until very light brown.
4. In a separate pan, boil the syrup until a few drops form a soft ball in cold water; dip each ear into this hot syrup and place on a large platter to cool.

Makes about one dozen.
– Mrs. Alvin LeJeune

# SYRUP CAKE

1 tsp. baking soda
1 1/2 cups cane syrup
2 eggs
1/2 cup cooking oil
3 cups flour

1 tsp. cinnamon
1/2 tsp. nutmeg
3 tbsp. sugar
3/4 cup milk

1. Mix together soda and syrup in a bowl; beat until creamy and light, as well as yellow in color.
2. Beat in eggs and oil. Combine flour, spices and sugar and blend well; add to syrup mixture alternately with milk.
3. Grease and flour a 13 x 9-inch baking pan. Pour batter into prepared pan and bake at 350 degrees for 35 to 40 minutes.
– Pat Gotte

# OLD-FASHIONED PECAN PRALINES

1 cup brown sugar
1 cup white sugar
1/2 cup evaporated milk
1/2 stick butter

Pinch salt
1 1/2 cups chopped or whole pecans
2 tbsp. vanilla

1. Mix together brown sugar, white sugar, milk, butter, and salt. Bring to a boil over medium heat.
2. Add pecans and cook to soft-ball stage (236 degrees on a candy thermometer). Mixture will be thick and hold together when stirred.
3. Remove from heat and add vanilla. Stir until mixture begins to dull in color and starts to thicken.
4. Working quickly, drop by spoonfuls onto waxed paper.
– Kit Johnson

# WHITE PECAN PRALINES

1 2/3 cups sugar
1 (5-oz.) can evaporated
  milk

12 large marshmallows
2 cups whole or broken pecans,
  (not chopped)
1/4 tsp. vanilla

1. Boil sugar and evaporated milk for 5 minutes.
2. Add marshmallows and stir until melted. Add pecans and vanilla.
3. Remove from heat and beat until mixture begins to thicken.
4. Working quickly, drop by spoonfuls onto waxed paper.
Makes about 24 pieces.
– Marie Watson

# DEWBERRY CAKE

Berry Mixture (Recipe follows)
1/2 cup butter, softened
1 cup sugar
2 eggs
2 cups flour
3 tsp. baking powder

1 tsp. salt
1 cup milk
1 tsp. vanilla
3/4 cup berry juice, reserved for
  top of cake

1. Prepare Berry Mixture; set aside.
2. Cream butter and sugar; beat in eggs.

3. Combine flour, baking powder and salt; add to creamed mixture alternately with milk and vanilla.
4. Pour batter into a greased 13 x 9-inch pan.
5. Pour Berry Mixture into batter and blend together.
6. Bake at 375 degrees for about 45 minutes or until a toothpick inserted near center comes out clean.
7. Drizzle extra berry juice over top of cake.

### BERRY MIXTURE

| | |
|---|---|
| 1 1/2 cups sugar | 3 to 4 cups dewberries or |
| 1 tbsp. cornstarch | blackberries |

1. Combine sugar and cornstarch in a medium saucepan and mix well.
2. Add dewberries and mix well.
3. Cook over medium heat until thickened, stirring constantly.
– Sue Schwartz

# MOLASSES POPCORN BALLS

| | |
|---|---|
| 1/2 cup molasses | 1/4 tsp. salt |
| 1/4 cup water | 1 1/4 tbsp. butter |
| 1/4 tsp. vinegar | 1 whole bag unsalted, unbuttered |
| 1/2 cup sugar | microwave popcorn, popped |

1. In a small saucepan, combine molasses, water, vinegar, sugar and salt.
2. Cook slowly, stirring once halfway through to scrape sugar off bottom. Cook until small quantity dropped in water forms threads.
3. Remove from heat, add butter and stir only enough to mix.
4. Put popcorn in a large bowl; pour mixture over popcorn, stirring constantly.
5. With buttered hands, quickly shape into balls.
6. Tip: If necessary, wrap balls in plastic wrap to help hold their form until cooled.
NOTE: Molasses is inclined to cling to the cup, or spoon that you will use to measure with. It will flow easier and will not cling if you grease the measure, or rinse it in cold water.
– Tony Chachere
*Tony Chachere's Cajun Country Cookbook*

# INDEX

# About The Author

Neal Bertrand was born and reared in Opelousas, Louisiana, in the heart of Cajun Country. He was the owner of a printing business for several years. He has more than a decade of experience in the publishing business. He is the publisher and owner of Cypress Cove Publishing in Lafayette, Louisiana.

**Books he has published for himself and others are:**
- Down-Home Cajun Cooking Favorites
- Rice Cooker Meals: Fast Home Cooking for Busy People
- Slow Cooker Meals: Easy Home Cooking for Busy People
- A House for Eliza: The Real Story of the Cajuns,
- Never Say Goodbye: Real Stories of the Cajuns,
- Cajun Country Fun Coloring & Activity Book (bi-lingual English/French)
- From Cradle to Grave: Journey of the Louisiana Orphan Train Riders
- Dad's War Photos: Adventures in the South Pacific
- Creative Writing Competition Winners 2012-2014: An Anthology from the Writers' Guild of Acadiana (Lafayette, Louisiana)

All of his books, rice cookers and other products can be seen and ordered from his websites, www.CypressCovePublishing.com, www.RiceCookerMeals.com, and www.DadsWarPhotos.com

You can contact and follow Neal on his blog at www.CypressCovePublishing.com

Watch his videos at www.youtube.com/user/cookbookdude

# Finally, a rice cooker with a stainless steel inner bowl!

Take your *Rice Cooker Meals* cooking to a new level of health and efficiency! Introducing our incredible, new 8-cup *Miracle* brand Stainless Steel Rice Cooker and Steamer!

- Cooks your meal automatically and then switches to a "stay-warm" mode when meal is fully cooked, keeping food warm for hours.
- This 8-cup cooker will yield a full 12 cups of cooked white or brown rice.
- The inner cooking pot is a beautiful solid mirror-finish stainless steel.
- The glass lid allows you to view the rice or vegetables while cooking.
- The stainless steel steaming tray fits on top of pot so you can steam vegetables to perfection (like yummy corn-on-the-cob) while cooking your meal.
- The easy view indicator lights identify cooking and warming cycles.
- Rice measuring cup and stirring paddle included for your convenience.
- 500 watts, 120 volts, 60 Hz

$79.95

Order yours today!

See Order Form

## DOWN-HOME CAJUN COOKING FAVORITES, REVISED SECOND EDITION

*Now even better!* A collection of classic recipes from the south Louisiana region called Acadiana, or Cajun Country. They were contributed by area folks who are tremendous cooks in their own right, who learned how to cook these dishes passed down from generation to generation. You'll find a variety of sauce piquantes, fricassees, stews, casseroles, appetizers, desserts, dressings, breads and breakfast dishes like *couche-couche* and *pain perdu.* Written in clear, easy-to-follow steps. Go ahead, try them, and you, too, will cook like a Cajun! 140 recipes, 102 pages, 6 x 9 soft cover, only $12.95.

## SLOW COOKER MEALS: EASY HOME COOKING FOR BUSY PEOPLE

Preparing a home-cooked meal in your slow cooker is delicious, nutritious, economical and easy. Put it on before you leave in the morning and it's cooked when you return. Loaded with easy meals anyone can fix, this cookbook includes Cajun meals such as jambalayas & pastalayas, sauce piquantes, étouffées, plus a large variety of soups, stews, and gumbos. It has poultry and meat dishes such as brisket, roasts, ribs and Cajun Pepper Steak. It has classics like chili and meat loaf. Also includes 17 desserts such as cobblers, puddings, fudge, peanut clusters and chocolate cake.

127 recipes, 96 pages, 6 x 9 soft cover, only $12.95.

## RICE COOKER MEALS: FAST HOME COOKING FOR BUSY PEOPLE

Fast, easy meals you can cook in a rice cooker; most have a 30-minute cook time. Convenient one-pot cooking means less mess to clean, easier to have good home cooking; less expensive and healthier than "fast-food". Great for busy people, college students, tailgating parties, campers, RV'ers, etc. Has 60 recipes to cook delicious pastas, seafood, soups, potatoes, cabbage, sweet potatoes, jambalayas and rice side dishes. Includes Mexican, Italian, Tex-Mex and Cajun recipes. 96 pages, 6 x 9 soft cover, only $12.95.

# ORDER FORM

For Autographed copies Call (337) 224-6576 or 888-606-3257.
For multiple copies call us to save money on shipping.
See all our books at www.CypressCovePublishing.com
All major credit cards are accepted
**Mail**   Complete form below and mail with check, money order or credit card authorization to:
**Cypress Cove Publishing**
908 Amilcar Blvd.
Lafayette, LA 70501

Please RUSH me:

| QTY | TITLE | Price | S & H |
|---|---|---|---|
| ____ | *Slow Cooker Meals: Easy Home Cooking for Busy People* | $12.95 | $3.50 |
| ____ | *Rice Cooker Meals: Fast Home Cooking for Busy People* | $12.95 | $3.50 |
| ____ | *Down-Home Cajun Cooking Favorites (Revised 2nd Ed.)* | $12.95 | $3.50 |
| ____ | *Cajun Country Fun Coloring & Activity Book* | $4.95 | $3.50 |
| ____ | Dad's War Photos: Adventures in the South Pacific | $19.95 | $3.50 |
| ____ | 8-cup Stainless Steel Rice Cooker | $79.95 | $15.00 |

Note: Rice Cooker sent by UPS. Please give your street address for Rice Cooker delivery. UPS cannot deliver to PO boxes. Thanks!

❑ Makes a great gift! If you are buying for someone beside yourself (or in addition to yourself), please check here and write the name and address of the recipients on a separate sheet of paper.

❑ Enclosed is my check or money order for $ _____
Please make check or money order payable to **Cypress Cove Publishing**.

❑ Charge $ _____    ❑ Visa ❑ MasterCard ❑ AmEx ❑ Discover

Card # _____ Exp. Date ____ / ____ 3-digit code _____

Signature _____

Name _____

Address _____

City, State, ZIP _____

Phone _____ email _____

*Thank you for your business!*

CPSIA information can be obtained
at www.ICGtesting.com
Printed in the USA
FFOW02n2337110718
47403512-50558FF